Rev. Francis R. Davis
Our Lady Of Lourdes
120 Fairmont Road
Elmira, N. Y. 14905

HANGING IN THERE
WITH CHRIST

HANGING IN THERE WITH CHRIST

by Robert J. Waywood O.F.M.

FRANCISCAN HERALD PRESS
Chicago, Illinois 60609

Hanging In There With Christ by Robert J. Waywood O.F.M. originally appeared as articles in *The Cord*, monthly review published by the Franciscan Institute of St. Bonaventure University. Copyright © 1974 Franciscan Herald Press, 1434 West 51st St., Chicago, Illinois 60609. Made in the United States of America.

Library of Congress Cataloging in Publication Data

Waywood, Robert J.
  Hanging in there with Christ.

  1. Spiritual life—Catholic authors. I. Title.
BX2350.2.W38   248'.48'2   74-1367
ISBN 0-8199-0498-8

Nihil Obstat:
  Mark Hegener O.F.M.
  Censor Deputatus

Imprimatur:
  Msgr. Richard A. Rosemeyer, J.D.
  Vicar General, Archdiocese of Chicago

April 15, 1974

"The Nihil Obstat and the Imprimatur are official declarations that a book or pamphlet is free of doctrinal or moral error. No implication is contained therein that those who have granted the Nihil Obstat and Imprimatur agree with the contents, opinions, or statements expressed."

Contents

Foreword vi

1. The Greatness of Gratitude 1

2. Four Cheers for Cheerfulness 7

3. The Wonderful World of Work 15

4. Merciful Heavens! 25

5. Putting Faith into Focus 35

6. Hounds of Heaven 51

7. Amazing Communication 65

8. The Charms of Chastity 80

9. Super Supper 102

10. Last Things First 114

Foreword

On this preliminary page, I want to present a brief justification of the content, order, and title of these collected conferences. When I rashly promised the lean and hungry editor of *The Cord*, Fr. Michael D. Meilach, O.F.M., that I would supply him with Franciscan spiritual fodder for the year 1972, I was resolved to crank out some readable and slightly inspirational prose—but on just what unprofane subjects I wasn't then perfectly clear. I knew, *saltem in confuso*, that I would focus on matters essential, not precious (like the six petals of the mystical rose), incontrovertible, not tendentious (like the value of blind obedience), and timely, not academic (like the methodology of mental prayer). Granting these guidelines, I would not exactly evade my "pet" spiritual topics, either—like work and Heaven.

The uneven length, the inconsistent tone, and the variegated matter of the following chapters may lead the reader to believe he is holding a glaring example of second-hand manuscript. I can only plead that the original conferences were flippant or formal, sketchy or exhaustive, short and simple or long and labyrinthine as the subject dictated. As these chapters now stand, they betray a deft, if subtle, order of sequence. The first four chapters consider important *prolegomena* of spirituality—natural pillars, so to speak, of supernatural sanity: the goodness of God and the worthwhileness of life. The next two conferences move on to higher realms—the keeping and the sharing of the Faith. In chapters seven through nine, I have tried to describe the supernatural lifelines I think need emphasizing for today's religious: prayer, chastity, and the Mass. The last chapter, logically, treats of the Last Things.

As for my colloquial title, I chose it for more than its catchiness and modernity. Hanging in there with Christ—an image which hits the nail on the head—implies that conditions are such today in the world, in the Church, and especially in the religious life, that simply to hold ground is heroic, just to persevere is excruciating, mere survival is a monumental achievement. The purpose of this book and the prayer of the author is that each reader may more easily and more eagerly identify with Christ and him crucified.

HANGING IN THERE
WITH CHRIST

1. *The Greatness of Gratitude*

IT WAS ONLY natural that Jesus should have miraculously multiplied the loaves in the desert, for he was a supernatural Person. It is not entirely puzzling that thereafter he should command the leftover morsels to be collected, for he was human like us in every feature except sinfulness. What is a bit astounding is that Jesus should so manifestly pause to give thanks for the provisions when he was himself the provider. Here as elsewhere Jesus was scrupulous in the observance of table prayers. The reason was, I believe, that the Master was furnishing his disciples with object lessons in a virtue that could bridge the human and the divine, that could most expeditiously lead man to God: the virtue of gratitude.

Twelve centuries after this miracle, the scene has changed from a grassy hill in the wilderness of Galilee to the dusty outskirts of a town in southern France. Saint Francis, who was neither photogenic in feature nor impressive in stature, and Brother Masseo, who could have filled any casting-director's bill as the "tall, dark, and handsome type," had just returned from their daily quest for bread. Francis exhibited his fistful of crumbs, and Brother Masseo appeared with several long loaves of bread tucked under his arms. On hearing the Saint chortle, "Brother Masseo, we're not worthy of such rich treasures as these," the good-looking friar wryly remarked, "Father, how can you talk of treasure when we lack just about everything! We don't have a table or knives or plates or beverage—just a few chunks of stale bread." Saint

Francis jubilantly rejoined, "This is the very reason why I consider our meal a great treasure, because man has hardly had a hand in it, but all has been bestowed by divine Providence—as we clearly see in this bread of charity, this beautiful table of stone, and this clear stream of water. And so, let us beg God to make us love with all our hearts the treasure of holy poverty." Thereupon Francis devoutly gave thanks, and both men fell to the bread with gusto.

Obviously, poverty was the leading virtue, not to say *idée fixe*, of the man nicknamed "the Poverello." Most of his other moral excellencies are easily reducible to poverty. His remarkable humility—his sincerely low esteem of himself—was due to a sort of poverty of mind. His legendary obedience in regard to ecclesiastical authorities, religious superiors, and his own holy Rule may be construed as a certain poverty of will. Actually, his poverty might itself be further reduced to, and explained by, his habitual attitude of gratitude. It was precisely this grateful frame of mind, which lay at the root of his poverty, that distinguished Francis from a hundred and one ordinary beggars of Assisi and from the elite religious fanatics, such as the Albigenses, of the thirteenth century. Necessary poverty without gratitude is chill penury or greedy destitution; voluntary poverty without gratitude is gaunt and grumbling asceticism. But poverty with and because of gratitude is Holy Poverty—perfect joy, in the eyes of Saint Francis.

If there was one man who could understand and articulate the outlook and uplook of the grateful beggar of Assisi, it was his biographer Gilbert Keith Chesterton. In several essays touching upon the Saint, Chesterton explained Franciscan gratitude. It might be likened to that giddy and grateful surprise Robinson Crusoe experienced upon salvaging a small but valuable miscellany from the recent wreck. Each precious item—the axe, the fowling-piece, the roll of lead, the sodden gunpowder—was affectionately gathered and thoughtfully

The Greatness of Gratitude

catalogued at the water's brink. So too, Saint Francis regarded all the creatures under the sun with fierce endearment and spontaneous appreciation as if rescued by Jesus Christ from the cosmic shipwreck that was Original Sin.

Chesterton further elaborated the Franciscan mentality when he posed the question in his *Autobiography*, "Who am I that I should deserve a dandelion?" The query plainly re-echoed the Poverello's ecstatic interrogation, "Lord, who am I but a miserable little worm?" Elsewhere Chesterton reasoned that, if children thank their parents on Christmas morning for filling their stockings with sweetmeats, parents ought to thank God every morning for filling their children's stockings with . . . legs—the latter being no less gratuitous than the former. Such was the sentiment of Saint Francis when he regarded Sister Water, who was usually taken for granted instead of taken with gratitude:

> *Be praised, my Lord, for Sister Water,*
> *rolling or running in a whirl—*
> *To Thee, a chaste, devoted daughter;*
> *to man, a humble servant girl.*

Canticle of the Sun

Chesterton, following suit, suggested that we compose and offer a grace before opera and a grace before work to complement our grace before meals. His secretary of many years, Dorothy Thompson, testifies that Chesterton used to make a sign of the Cross with his cigar before lighting up. Francis had gone even further with his gratitude and recited a grace before being cauterized with a hot iron.

With such a weight of testimony to recommend it, this virtue of gratitude bears looking into more closely. Thanksgiving has always been reckoned as one of the aims of the believer's prayer to God; but the philosopher, I think, would do well to study the phenomenon of gratitude as an argument in itself for belief in God. The argument no doubt can be analyzed as being merely an application of the proof of God's existence from causality. But its appeal transcends the purely notional and penetrates to the visceral level. Oscar Wilde once quipped that people do not really appreciate a beautiful sunset because they cannot pay for it. Chesterton had a ready answer to that cynical stance: he said that people could pay for that satisfying sight by not being other Oscar Wildes, that is, by not being as cynical and amoral as the decadent poet. But a more immediate reaction to, and recompense for, the view of a gorgeous sunset is simply to enjoy it in grateful awe. Whether gratitude be experienced as a sentiment or a sensation, like love, it is meaningless when looked upon absolutely—as occurring in a vacuum—and without relationship to another person. To give thanks or even to feel like giving thanks implies a person to receive the thanks. And when the gratuity bestowed obviously has no human referent, as would be the case with a thrilling vista of the Grand Canyon or a startling panorama of the stars, the terminus of the thanks must be another Person—capital *P*. The most ridiculous sight in the world has to be an atheist atop the Matterhorn gaping at the inspiring spectacle below.

Like the philosopher, the psychologist will discover in the exercise of gratitude something elementary and advantageous. There is something radically therapeutic, for the sick mind and the tortured will, in a spontaneous act of thanksgiving. Gratitude puts things in accurate perspective: as when a man measures his shoddy footwear against the amputee's indigence. And, as a smile (physiologists say) relaxes and refreshes the facial muscles with negligible effort, so a grateful sigh gratuitously unstrings the harried or scruple-ridden heart. Many a counselor has bidden his client count his little blessings—like indoor plumbing and gainful employment—to invite repose. Awareness of larger, if less obvious, gifts such as the breath of life or the memory of a mother, can make him bolt from his early morning bed and dash to his duties. The grateful neurotic is well on the road to recovery. He is miles ahead of the somber soul who decrees with fearful effrontery, "Blessed are those who expect nothing, for they shall not be disappointed."

The serious student of asceticism will find in gratitude a virtue worthy of close consideration and unqualified cultivation. On the one hand, the exercise of thanksgiving can never become excessive. Hope pushed too far can turn into presumption; faith can be contorted into superstition; prudence in excess can beget paralysis; fortitude in the extreme becomes recklessness; even temperance and justice have their outer limits. But gratitude, like the charity Saint Paul describes in the thirteenth chapter of his first Letter to the Corinthians, cannot be overdone. On the other hand, the practice of the virtue of gratitude is safely within the reach of everyone, whatever his spiritual stature or ethical propensities. Very few can emulate the flaming faith, the iron fortitude, or the excruciating poverty of a Saint Francis of Assisi. But no one has to shrink from or strain after the example of gratitude left us by the Poverello. Even the moral back-slider can be Christ-like to the extent of mumbling his table prayers into his beer.

As a follower of Saint Francis who has—thank God—an ear for music, I have often mused what might make a good theme song for the Franciscan Order. Some titles immediately came to mind; "I've Got Plenty of Nothing," for example, or "The Best Things in Life Are Free." On further consideration, however, it occurred to me that probably the most appropriate number was the Chant Preface in the Missal. The start of that song, I think, makes a fitting close for this explanation of the greatness of gratitude. It goes: "Father, all-powerful and ever-living God, we do well always and everywhere to give you thanks . . . ."

A Rousing Rhapsody

God be praised for all things sturdy, staunch, and stout:
        Things stirring-strong, invisible within;
        Things stolid, solid, palpable without.
God be praised for thick white milk, for strong amber ale;
        For friendship's stouter hand-shake partings,
        For fellow comrades' quickening, hearty "Hail".
God be praised for solid oak trees, for sturdy girders;
        For fortitude's firm, straining self-refusals,
        For patience's puissant egotism murders.
God be praised for all squat houses and tall towers;
        For Faith's fast footing treading granite dogmas,
        For Hope's hale help in dark, dank hours.

2. Four Cheers for Cheerfulness

EVERY SON AND daughter of Saint Francis has four solid reasons for floating on Cloud Number Nine, that is, for being perpetually cheerful. Before we get to those reasons, I had better apologize briefly for even broaching the subject of cheerfulness. For to devote a whole conference, and just at this time, to cheerfulness well may strike you as whimsical and inopportune. The virtue hardly seems central to Christian ethics or ascetics. You will look for it in vain among the three theological virtues, the four cardinal virtues, the six precepts of the Church, the seven Gifts of the Holy Spirit, the eight Beatitudes, or the Ten Commandments. And the imagery generated by today's headlines—napalm, botulism, rubber bullets, skyjacking, environmental pollution, and clerical defection—leaves little room in your head for visions of sugarplums. Nevertheless, the virtue of cheerfulness is both paramount and relevant.

In the sixth chapter of Ephesians, Saint Paul makes the terrifying revelation that we stumbling sons of Adam are actually caught up in a cosmic conflict, that "our wrestling is not against flesh and blood . . . but against the spiritual forces of wickedness on high." Then he lists the Christian's arsenal for waging that war: truth, justice, faith, the Word of God. These, indeed, are the weapons and armor for the spiritual combat that is life. But with the advent of mass media and the growth of international awareness, the tactics of that age-old battle, I think, have taken a new turn and call for updated defenses. Nowadays we understand the critical importance of morale and the insidious effectiveness of psychological warfare. And nowadays every morning newspaper or evening news telecast—droning an endless drama of outrageous crimes, lurid atrocities, natural calamities, and horrendous mistakes—may be construed as propaganda leaflets strewn by the Enemy. If discouragement is in the air, and if that mood is the prelude to despair, and if despair is the ultimate sin, then certainly you can see the unprecedented importance of maintaining good spirits, of cultivating cheerfulness. Cheerfulness is the most powerful static we have to cope with Axis Charley's propaganda.

Granting, then, that the topic is timely and significant, let us consider what grounds we have to remain securely steeped in good cheer. We hold four separate titles to the right to be merry: as believers in God, as disciples of Christ, as associates of the Saints, and as followers of Saint Francis.

If we say that we believe in God, we have said a mouthful. For to assent to the existence of a Supreme Being is to assert unconditionally that a whole spectrum of divine attributes is operative, much to the believer's consolation. If we fail to appreciate fully this source of encouragement, namely, the consideration of God's attributes, it is probably because we let our imagination get in the way or play tricks on us, thus anthropomorphizing his immutability, omniscience, or omnipotence. For example, all of us have had at least one rapturous moment in our lives, maybe standing beneath the stars, surprised by the grandeur of nature, or sitting in a cozy chair after closing a thrilling novel, a lucid interval, when we instinctively, wordlessly, praised the First Cause and mused on his serene benignity—and the deductions of theodicy would fully substantiate our intuition of the moment. But later, in a more pedestrian hour, soured by a dose of *Weltschmerz* or groping our way through the vagaries of Salvation History, we envisioned God as a grim-faced monitor of the world scene or a petulant, if ultimately patient, taskmaster of the Chosen People. Mercurial mortals that we are, we have forgotten for the nonce what philosophy and Scripture aver about the Deity, "with whom there is no change, nor shadow of alteration" (James 1:17). Again, we are intellectually convinced that God is all-knowing, familiarity with genetic codes and giant computers only buttressing that conviction; yet our imagination staggers over the knowledge explosion, the Sunday New York Times, the hopelessly involved Pentagon Papers, and conditions us to regard the All-seeing Eye with a somewhat arched eyebrow. We palpably doubt sometimes that God can really be on top of the situation. And although we notionally concede that God is all-powerful, our panic and paralysis in the face of the ongoing human tragedy argue to the fact that we have practically reverted to Zoroastrianism, with its belief in equiposed good and evil deities.

If we allow our imagination to dwindle these attributes of God, we are selling short a chief cause for cheerfulness. For do what we may, feel how we will, God is supremely, immutably, unconditionally happy. And the saga of disappointments mankind has presented him has not made the slightest diminution of his good spirits. God, who could be defined as the only person who never has to eat his words, still looks upon all that he has made and opines that it is "very good." Every newborn baby is evidence that God has not swept aside the whole scheme as a bad experiment. Among us mortals good spirits are, fortunately, as contagious as depression. Remember how in Robert Browning's poem "Pippa Passes" a little factory girl on vacation uplifted the gloomy and anxious hearts of those who overheard her simple song:

> *The year's at the spring,*
>   *The day's at the morn,*
> *Morning's at seven,*

The hillsides dew pearled.
The lark's on the wing,
The snail's on the thorn,
God's in his heaven—
All's right with the world.

If we set ourselves to seriously contemplating God's celestial levity, some of it is bound to rub off.

As disciples of Jesus Christ we should be cheerful. Now, considering that the Master appears as a decidedly grave man in all four Gospels, perhaps this conclusion is not immediately evident. But you must bear in mind that the Evangelists were bent upon writing a selective interpretation, not a facsimile account, of the life of Jesus. (In fact, not until Boswell's life of Samuel Johnson appeared in the eighteenth century was there any such thing as an all-round, realistic biography to be read.) The words and deeds of Jesus before his Resurrection were all, understandably, colored by the shadow of the Cross. But even there, solemn as our Lord appears, his life still radiated a quiet kind of joy, and he did encourage cheerfulness in his disciples up to the very night of his Passion. Almost every time he returned to his Apostles after having left their midst for a while, he could be heard to exhort: "Do not be afraid," or "Be of good cheer." If we may believe a scholar like Father Sloyan, Jesus was not above making and playing jokes (like so many entertainers of Jewish descent). He dubbed James and John "sons of Thunder" probably because their father Zebedee let rip a few curses when the Master had coaxed them away from their boat and nets to make them fishers of men. Speaking of Herod the Less, Jesus called him a fox and bade him (in the Aramaic equivalent) to go "whistle 'Dixie.' " As for playing tricks on his followers, remember how Jesus asked baited questions like, "Who touched me?" when a crowd had thronged around him close as sardines; or, "where will we buy bread?" when they were out in the boondocks. The playful good cheer bubbles up more evidently after the Resurrection, for example, when Jesus "strung along" the two disciples for the duration of a five-mile walk to Emmaus. Although Jesus could aptly be identified as the Man of Sorrows, his sermons, especially those on the Mount, were certainly calculated to rout human anxiety and gloom for all times. If the Master never relaxed into a full grin while on earth, maybe, as Chesterton has suggested, he is saving that heart-warming sight for the citizens of the New Jerusalem.

If Jesus himself was not noticeably ebullient, at least he urged his followers to be so. At the Last Supper, having assured the Apostles that in the world they would have affliction, he quickly added, "But take courage, I have overcome the world" (Jn. 16:33). And then, at the peak of his priestly prayer, he confessed: "These things I speak in the world, in order that they may have *my joy made full in themselves*" (Jn. 17:13). And the invitation to Christian cheerfulness was not wasted on that *alter Christus*, Saint Paul. After a lifetime of harrowing adventures and human disappointments, imprisoned and awaiting execution, the Apostle to the Nations practically lapsed into ecstasy when he wrote to the Philippians what amounts to a manifesto of Christian optimism and humanism: "Rejoice in the Lord always; again I say, rejoice . . . have no anxiety . . . and may the peace of God which surpasses all understanding guard your hearts and your minds" (Phil. 4:4-7). Yes, as followers of Christ, like Saint Paul, we have a right—no, a duty—to be cheerful.

Even a brief look at hagiography down through the checkered history of the Church should convince us that as companions of the Saints we have grounds to be cheerful. Just to cull a few examples, there is Blessed Julian, recluse of Norwich, according to whose *Revelations* Jesus reproached her in a lugubrious moment from the Crucifix, saying, "My daughter, you have every right to be merry as any great lady in the world." The doughty Teresa of Avila used to chide, "God deliver us from sour-faced saints!" A spirit of holy nonchalance pervades Saint Francis of Sales's delightful *Introduction to the Devout Life*. Saint Philip of Neri is reputed to have scanned joke books as part of his preparation for Mass—to bring his ecstatic spirits back to reality. Don Bosco's avowed mission was "to spread abroad the smile of religion." But perhaps the cheeriest Saint we have on record is statesman-martyr Thomas More. Ever a wit, Saint Thomas jested all the way to execution. Well acquainted with the guard of London Tower, Thomas chided the man, "If I complain about my accommodations here, don't hesitate to show me out." Mounting the scaffold, he bade the executioner to "give me a hand going up: coming down, I'll shift for myself." And just before the axe fell, he admonished the axeman to pull his beard out of the way of the blade for "that, at least, had not offended the King." If you wish to pursue this merry side of the Saints, you may read short but scintillating biographies of forty of them in Sheed and Ward's publication, *Saints Who Were Not Sad*.

But probably the most immediate title we hold to cheerfulness stems from our association with Saint Francis of Assisi. After the foggy pensiveness that preceded his conversion had passed, the Poverello's life proved to be filled with almost uninterrupted good cheer, whether he was fiddling an imaginary violin in the woods, chortling the latest stanza of his *Canticle of the Sun*, or bantering with his favorite follower, the clownish Brother Juniper. His manifest optimism was neither shallow nor evanescent; for it sprang from a rooted conviction that God was his Father, Jesus was his liege Lord, and creatures were his brothers. Perfect joy for him, as Brother Leo discovered, depended very little upon human comfort, security, or accomplishment. So he could jest when the glowing iron cauterized his eyes and graciously

Four Cheers for Cheerfulness

nibble Brother Jacoba's almond cakes on his death-bed. Saint Francis knew, too, the strategic importance of abiding cheerfulness. Some of his strongest words recommend that virtue to his disciples. We would do well to repeat them here, lengthy though they are:

> It is for the Devil to be sad, but for us always to be cheerful and happy in the Lord.
>
> If the servant of God studies to have and keep, within and without, that spiritual cheerfulness that proceeds from a clean heart and is acquired by devotion to prayer, the evil spirits cannot harm him.
>
> The Devil exults most when he can steal a man's joy of spirit from him. But when spiritual joy fills our hearts, the Serpent pours out his deadly poison in vain.
>
> The demons cannot hurt a servant of Christ when they see him filled with holy mirth.
>
> Why do you show your sorrow and sadness for your sins exteriorly? Keep such sadness between yourself and God, and pray that in his mercy he may pardon you and give you back the gladness of his salvation. But before me and the rest try always to have a cheerful air: it does not become a servant of God to appear before his brother or anybody else with sadness and a troubled countenance.

Thank heavens, most of the followers of Saint Francis have been chips off the old block, have been noticeably chipper souls.

From four points of view, then, we sons and daughters of Saint Francis are entitled to live our lives in relative good cheer, until we arrive where *every* tear shall be wiped away . . . . With a little stretch of the imagination, we might update that metaphor of the Big Book and think of our lives as being recorded on celestial video tape. Have you got the picture? Smile—you *are* on Candid Camera.

Bonum Est Diffusivum Sui

Once I lay upon the floor
In a balmy summer's gloom,
Listening to the radio pour
Music waves on rug and room.

So enchanting was the song,
So enthralling was the tune,
I could not remain there long;
I should have to share this boon.

I should have to fetch another
Before the song began again;
Rapt, I ran to bring my brother,
Both to bask in the warm refrain.

Joy cannot, like clinging pelf,
Lie imprisoned in a purse:
God could not contain Himself,
Had to make this universe.

3. The Wonderful World of Work

WHAT STARTED ME thinking about the more-than-workaday significance of work was an old book I spied gathering dust on a remote shelf of our seminary library. The burden of the book and the author's name escape me now, but the gilded title shines in my memory: *The Eighth Sacrament: Work*. Meditation on the topic since then has convinced me that Father Ignotus was not exaggerating. What engages half of our waking hours in this global hive really is replete with wonderful meaning. I can just begin to suggest the sacred significance of work by serving up a few points for your reflection. Upon analysis, work may be regarded as a penance, a preventative, a prayer, a performance, and a profit.

Only at rare intervals, while basking in the satisfaction of a job well done, or in retrospective retirement, when memory blurs the hard edges of reality, only then will we deny that our work is, all things considered, a pain in the neck. The onerous quality of employment was borne in on me early in life, when as a youngster I would lie awake weekday mornings (before my mother would rouse us for the second breakfast shift) and hear my father coughing in the astringent winter air as he cranked his gelid Essex to life. Several years later catechism class and basic Latin taught me the connection between the "pain" of painstaking labor and the "penalty" called down on our first parents.

Tending the Garden of Eden must have been "duck soup" before the Fall, but cultivating clods was decidedly "tough turkey" afterwards:

> *"When Adam delved and Eve she spun
> Who was then the gentleman?"*

Despite curious exceptions like gentlemen of leisure and knights of the road, the generality of mankind have verified the effectiveness of that primal curse, "By the sweat of your brow, you will eat your bread." Few of the world's workforce will disclaim that their job ultimately demands all the patience of a Job. It doesn't seem to matter what the nature of the job is. Even minding the store entails mental effort. Maybe there's no business like show business, but actresses who mean business like Barbara Stanwyck are always confiding to Sunday-supplement hacks that it's no bed of roses. Programmers may not slave like piece-workers, but they also serve who only stand and wait for printouts. And progress appears simply to have metamorphosed man's exertions or telescoped his toil. In *Future Shock* utopias silicosis and housemaid's knee are replaced by jet-lag and traffic-thrombosis. Even if the breadwinner of the twenty-fifth century has to don his white collar just one day a week, I feel sure that obnoxious decision-making and hypodermic head-scratching will make the dawning of that day unwelcome.

Yet it lies within man to recognize his travail as a punishment and to transmute it into a salutary penance for his and society's offenses against the Creator. Thus to accept and even embrace the irksome circumstances of labor is more than making the best of a bad situation: it is making the most of it. Regarding our work as a penalty attendant on Original Sin and as a penance for actual sin can make all our efforts constructive efforts, that is, re-constructive. When He was asked about the guilt of eighteen random citizens of Jerusalem crushed by the tower of Siloe, Jesus answered, "Unless you repent, you will all perish in the same manner" (Lk. 13:5). The summons is universal, for all have sinned. Without delving into all the implications of repentance, we

The Wonderful World of Work

can concede that it involves expiating forbidden satisfaction, redressing disobedience, and curbing excesses of the ego. Ideally, a penance should be appropriate, ready-made, and foolproof. What better penance, then, than the services of the vocation of our choice which simultaneously demand hardship, obligation, and self-effacement? No wonder the early Church actually assigned servile tasks as public penance, or that Pope John XXIII awarded a plenary indulgence for simply doing one's job for a month. Thankfully, the scripture that bids us work out our salvation is literally true; and this valley of tears is really the vestibule of Purgatory.

An ounce of prevention is worth a pound of cure. So work should be even more estimable because it helps us to avert sin as well as to atone for it. The adage about what constitutes the devil's workshop might be traceable to some parsimonious Puritan, but the sentiment behind it was the rule-of-thumb asceticism of the prodigal Poverello. On the subject of work, Saint Francis of Assisi spoke with all the emphasis of a broken record. In his two Rules and in various *dicta* he exhorted the brethren "to toil and exert themselves, lest, giving way to idleness, they stray into forbidden paths"; and he urged them "always to be doing some profitable work so that the devil might find them busy." I really believe that, on the great Come-And-Get-It Day, all flesh will see that billions of man-hours shall have done more to keep the bulk of humanity on the straight and narrow than centuries of sermons.

As a sin-preventative, work deserves some further analysis. Even if idleness were not the proverbial open invitation to temptation, it would still be a passport to sins of omission. This sprawling category of culpability has always had a tendency to remain subliminal in the human conscience. Thanks to the revised liturgy—that is, to the new form of the *Confiteor*, which gestures to "what we have failed to do," Catholics should be more aware of the invisible violence one can wreak just by killing time. Perhaps Horace Mann's entry in the imaginary Lost-Found column rings a little less corny to our ears now: "Lost, somewhere between sunrise and sunset, two golden hours, each set with sixty diamond minutes. No reward is offered, for they are gone forever."

But, let's face it, only two items in the Decalogue are expressed positively; so we are conditioned to think of transgressions as acts, not as non-acts. And usually what pricks our consciences is not some nebulous malaise over missed opportunities to do good, but crystal-clear instances of sins of commission. Speaking for myself, I confess that most of my regretful hours lie somewhere in the calendar of my off-hours. The mechanics of our mortal sins are not hard to fathom. For idleness is not a neutral state of affairs alas. Boredom or frustration is its inevitable concomitant. The bored man craves for a few kicks in life, and these often issue in the form of kicking over the traces. The frustrated man, even if he is a sage and a greybeard, can stoop momentarily to becoming a juvenile delinquent.

Feckless superstars become pedestrian playboys *off* the playing field. Virtuoso moviestars become common vandals when they step out of the klieglights into a nightclub. Accountants turn philanderers at weekend "wingdings," and burly bricklayers drink themselves to oblivion on their Friday paycheck. Obviously, professional pressures bear some causal relationship to these moral lapses. But I hardly think that a shrunken workweek or universal unemployment is the *sine qua non* of the sinless society. Even the jaded anti-clerical Voltaire admitted that work was prophylactic: he has disillusioned Candide voice the last words of wisdom: "Shut up, and cultivate your garden!" Putting your shoulder to the wheel, keeping your nose to the grindstone, and gluing your eyes on your work may be rough on the physique; but it does wonders for the soul's shape. Yes, by and large, the best buffer for temptation will always be work . . . and sleep.

So far this eulogy for useful employment may sound to you as if I'm reaching, trying desperately to make a virtue of a necessary evil. Well, let's consider work in a rosier light. Speaking positively, work is—or can be—a prayer. It is the only form of prayer that enables us to fulfill our Lord's injunction to "pray always and not lose heart." How work can be construed as prayer should be no more mysterious than the familiar phenomenon of, let's say, a draftsman dedicating his absorption with a blueprint to the wife and children smiling on his labors from the framed photograph on his desk. If, as Saint Paul has it, "God chose us in him [Jesus] before the foundation of the world, that we should be holy and without blemish in his sight and love" (Eph. 1:4), then we should understand that each of us really is working on "special assignment." Accepting and fulfilling that commission from our Chief Executive is communicating with God by intentional prayer. Good ascetical theology teaches us that actions which stem from and implement meditation constitute prayer, though certainly not the most intense degree of spiritual communication. Frankly, I've always thought that the catechism definition of prayer stood in need of revision. "Prayer is the uplifting"—I can see my mother menacing an uppercut to my brother as she rehearsed his lessons—"the uplifting of the mind and heart to God." It would be more accurate (and encouraging) to say that prayer is the uplifting of the mind and/or heart to God: sometimes the mind can't make it. Saint Paul is certainly commending the commonest sort of prayer when he tells us: "Whatsoever you do in word or in work, do all in the name of the Lord." Doing anything "in the name of the Lord" is pointing the heart, the affections, the intentions at God. Jesus didn't chase Martha out of the kitchen for her lack of devotion; he merely scolded her from the parlour for belittling Mary's more rapt attention to her Master.

To transmute the dross of toil to the gold of prayer, needless to say, requires some kind of deliberate consecration—candles are not necessary—of one's labors to the Lord and an occasional re-dedication. Similarly, that draftsman has to declare his love to the family and shoot a passing glance to the photo at work, or run the risk of having his priorities somersault and losing his family along with himself in his work. It would be scrupulous or superstitious to drive ourselves to distraction by mumbling ejaculations every quarter hour; but it would be perverse and unfeeling of us to be habitually forgetful of Whom we are working for.

Most people are normally a good deal more aware of whom they are working for than what they are working at. Whenever anyone asked my father, for instance, what he did for a living, Dad instinctively identified his employment with his management: "I'm with the M.D.C., Chestnut Hill Pumping Station." Except for the rarities who sign in on *What's My Line*, most of the gainfully employed think of themselves as agents rather than artisans. Just how much importance people place on their occupational connections can be overheard at introductory get-togethers. Miss So-and-so is a ghost-writer for Governor Rockefeller—though she works only part-time and hasn't eaten a square meal in a month. Professor What's-his-name functions at the Harvard School of Business—his subject is speed-typing. Mr. Whatchacallem is associated with Walt Disney Studios—he sketches in the four-fingered hands of Mickey and his gang. If we can thus sublimate our work naturally, why not supernaturally? It will divinely glamorize our efforts, improve our efficiency, and sweeten our toil to realize and avow that we are, at base, agents for the Almighty. Every time we formulate the morning offering we are punching our eternal time-clock, thereby making the daily grind turn into a prayer wheel that really works. I do believe that the road to *heaven* is paved, in this sense, with good intentions.

Work betrays more glorious potential when we look at it as

performance. Interestingly, I found the word "performance," a perfectly good synonym for work, lodged in *Roget's* in a list that included "fulfillment, accomplishment, achievement, flowering" (a narrower sense of the word situates it among music and drama terms). Before we see how well-performed work fulfills man, we should pause to remember how the lack of work can dehumanize a man. According to Victor Frankl, who knew whereof he spoke, the cruelest deprivation inflicted upon the inmates of German concentration camps was the absence of even penal chores. Without tasks whereby to orient their days, the prisoners who had been blue-collar workers and unused to mental gymnastics, virtually fell apart. Less lurid examples of this degeneracy lie closer to home in the form of a notorious welfare system, which turns able-bodied men into assorted creatures such as barflies and lounge-lizards, or in the shape of early retirement enforcement that transforms mature minds into TV vegetables and checker automatons. "I have seen the cedars of Lebanon fall," I mused to myself the day I heard my father—who had sailed the seven seas as a chief petty officer and worked hand in glove with Admiral King on torpedo warheads—give detailed biographies of every character blowing in and out of *Secret Storm*.

Work is so essential to the manness of man that every man-jack of us denominates himself by the job he plies. If you ask me who I am, off the top of my head, I reply, "A priest who teaches English." Just as I would not know who God was unless he had performed the works of creation, so I would be much in the dark as to my ego-identity without being able to refer to personal achievements in the realm of work.

Grant me a man that has carefully selected his life's vocation and made the skills of his trade or profession second nature; set him a challenging task and let him go to town. You will see man in his finest hour—whether making order out of a chaos of notes or conjuring up a radio from a heap of transistors. It was a thrill to see my father, a master machinist, in his prime: the monkey-wrench worked like an extension of his arm; his eyes were as accurate as calipers. That work galvanizes and potentiates human nature seems to be the central theme of the popular movie, *A Day in the Life of Ivan Denisovich*, itself a cinematic masterpiece for the glory of man and God. What but the challenge of work kept Shaw's tongue fluent, Toscanini's ear keen, Rubinstein's fingers nimble, and Einstein's imagination active? In his famous, spirited essay, "Aes Triplex," Robert Louis Stevenson, no shirker himself, claims that the Greeks had productive old age in mind as well as effervescent youth when they coined their proverb, "Those whom the gods love die young." Little wonder that work can often prove to be the apotheosis of man; for the Son of Man divulged: "My Father works even until now, and I work" (Jn. 5:16).

The real apotheosis of man, of course, will come in the afterlife. So let us, finally, address our attention to work as something supernaturally profitable. Certainly this is no place to review the theology of merit, the nature and conditions of heavenly reward—though I would like some time to give a piece of my mind on the subject to unrealistic Christians who preach earthly impotence and celestial equality, to idealistic Catholics who claim to be less ulteriorly motivated than the saints, and to simplistic Communists who can conceive of the *summum bonum* only as a baker's treat. Suffice it to say, Jesus assures us that there is a way to store up moth-repellent, rust-resistant, burglar-proof wealth in the next world. This side of the grave, eye has not seen nor ear heard the quality or quantity of that reward. As to how we go about amassing these eternal earnings, our Lord is far from vague: we are to love God and our neighbor; we are to keep the Commandments; we are to practice the works of mercy. Everyone knows that the two great Commandments are a resolution of the Ten Commandments, but the works of mercy may seem a bit exotic and extraordinary—to be coterminous with the Decalogue and utterly unrelated to the work that consumes the half of one's waking hours. But properly understood, that catalogue by which our eternal destiny will be determined is intimately connected with our ethics and our work. I can illustrate the point more succinctly than I can explain it.

The story goes that a pastor had carefully banked the collection for decades to finance the building of a sorely needed new church building. Most of the details of the edifice, he had wisely left in the hands of the architect. But he had penned instructions as to what the six nave windows were to depict, their theme being the works of mercy. Actually, he died before ground was broken, and the windows eventually featured garish portraits of popular saints. So you will look in vain for these stained-glass tributes to the corporal works of mercy.

According to the padre's instructions, the first window was to show a little, old lady stowing cans of Campbell's soup in a wire cart. The second was to display a begrimed plumber half-way out of a manhole. The third was to feature a nurse adjusting a blanket in an incubator ward. The fourth (as you genuflect and move to the epistle side) was to highlight a young housewife stuffing laundry into a Westinghouse washer. The fifth was to enshrine a dentist plying a drill in a teenager's mouth. And the sixth was to portray two policemen in a patrol car parked beside a traffic light.

The old pastor was right. For our terrestrial tedium more than any other endeavor qualifies us for life everlasting and is, in fact, holy work. What begins as a penance ends as a premium. The ancient proverb is, eschatologically speaking, the stark and startling truth: *Per aspera ad astra*, through hardships to the stars!

Trinity of Day

Morning is a garden
Where the sky is full of song
And a fragrance fills the land.
God walks in the garden
And throughout the morning long
I take the Father's hand.

Noontide is a forum
Where the sun is blazing down
On a motley crowd and mixed.
Man is in the forum,
But just outside the town
I see the Christ transfixed.

Evening is a prairie
Where the purple clouds creep lowly
And earth's silence is a thunder.
Prayer roves in the prairie
While I lie and let the Holy
Spirit fold me under.

4. Merciful Heavens!

A LITTLE REFLECTION on our moral vocabulary will show that there is only a hair's-breath difference between "godly" and "snobbish" in the popular mind. Take the word "moral" itself. The adjective derived from it—"moralistic"—is fraught with supercilious overtones. And while piety may still pass as a noble quality of soul, most of us would rather cross the street than run into a pietistic soul. To be always in the right and to be righteous are horses that are sometimes of indistinguishable hue. Most people would no more wish to be accused of sanctity than they would of being sanctimonious. Anyone who is noticeably pure stands in danger of being tagged as puritanic. Accordingly, most people are actually bragging when they confess, "I'm no *saint*." They are inclined to shoot holes through a reputation of holiness and to mistake a halo for a high hat. Instinctively they feel that even an obviously good man is not all he's "cracked up to be."

On the other hand, the populace are just as eager to "give the devil his due." I mean, we have only to scan the plots of pulp literature (and even those of a good deal of gilt-edged fiction) to see the popularity of the vulnerable protagonist or the less-than-lily-white heroine. The gallery of literature is crowded with kindly rogues and winsome wenches. From Henry Fielding to Graham Greene, from *Moll Flanders* to *Suzie Wong*, hosts of clay-footed characters have marched through our native fiction: the prostitute with a heart of gold, the alcoholic doctor or pastor with tear-drenched shoulders, the mother-loving mobster, the prince charming who goes from pillow to pillow in search of his abducted fiancee, the dance-hall doxy who is putting her brother through medical school, and the racketeer who puts rum-dum ex-boxers on the payroll.

The tendency to see every white thing as a whited sepulchre is simplistic and prejudicial beyond a doubt. And the penchant to believe that the devil is not so black as he is painted is subject to maudlin exaggeration. Prescinding from excesses, there is, nevertheless, something healthy and elemental underlying these two ethical attitudes. By the end of this conference I hope to have spelled out what that something is. Be that as it may, at face value it seems scandalous to maintain that saints are villains and sinners are heroes. But then, there was in history a religious founder who taught almost as much and as a result became a scandal to the Jews and a stumbling-block to the gentiles. If there had been a tabloid newspaper in the days of Jesus of Nazareth, say, *The Jerusalem Journal* (with "all the news that's fit to print" . . . and then some), the headlines would have read in large, lurid lines: HARLOTS FLOCK TO NEW PREACHER-MAN or RABBI ROOMS WITH ROBBERS or CARPENTER PUTS DOWN HIGHPRIEST. Christ's outlook on matters sacred and profane may ultimately have proven healthy and elemental, but in his day it was definitely unsettling and sensational. Let us now take a long look at the Master's treatment of sinners in general and in particular.

We know full well what the general mission of the Godman was in this world. We know it on his own admission: "It is not the healthy who need a physician, but they who are sick. I have not come to call the just, but sinners, to repentance" (Lk. 5:31-32). A swift survey of his works and words will demonstrate that he earned the "mission accomplished" medal. Immediately after Peter dropped his chin to his chest and warned Jesus not to risk his reputation associating with a wharf-rat like himself, the Lord drafted the fisherman into service aboard his spiritual barque. Jesus fished for his own kind of soul-food at a well side and gently "hooked" a prize catch, the town trollop. He healed body and soul of both the young paralytic let down through the roof and the old paralytic stretched out beside the pool. He publicly defended and privately pardoned a wife who had been caught in the act of making love with her boyfriend. He condoned and apologized for his disciples who out of human weakness had picked and eaten some ears of wheat in violation of strict Sabbath observance. He acknowledged and saluted the repentance of a woman of ill repute who had slipped into Simon the Pharisee's banquet. And finally, he invited a thief, turned honest-to-God, to accompany him into Paradise. This is a mere summary of the Master's treatment of sinners as actually recorded in the Scriptures. Doubtless, the full chronicle of the God-man who would not quench the smoldering wick or break the bruised reed would include many further feats of forgiveness. But we have here enough evidence to see the general pattern of the Savior's behavior: he not only rubs out the record for self-confessed sinners; in doing so, he often "rubs it in" for self-proclaimed saints.

If this kind of conduct drew a raised eyebrow from the professional holy men of the day, the Master's parables fairly set their ears ringing. The analogies involving a strayed sheep or a lost silverpiece were bad enough—headlining as they did God's delight over the evildoer's conversion. The chiaroscuro cameo that contrasts the arrogant Pharisee and the humbled publican was worse—after all, wasn't the disciple of Moses doing all the right things? But the detailed narrative of the Prodigal Son . . . that was the last straw! This upstart Rabbi was being unconscionable. In this short story not only does a wiseacre young whippersnapper turn out to be the hero (co-featured with his merciful father); but also the older son, a God-fearing pillar of the community who always toed the mark and kept his nose to the grindstone, comes close to evolving into a whimpering self-righteous villain of the piece. From a purely natural point of view this eventuality seems a bit much. If the parable savors of the melodramatic, maybe that was the only way Jesus could dramatize the mercy of God.

His adversaries little dreamed what a compliment they were handing Jesus, or what a mouthful they were saying, when they charged him with being a friend of sinners: "Behold a man who is a glutton and a wine-drinker, a friend of publicans and sinners!"(Lk. 7:34). Let us see in particular if what they said was true—if Jesus really did befriend, sweetly convert, and exquisitely employ people with noticeable human frailties. To be systematic about it, let us recall and apply the catalogue of vices known as the seven capital sins: pride, greed, lust, anger, envy, gluttony, and sloth. We can easily find a victim of each of these vices in the Lord's circle of friends.

None of the Apostles seems at the start to have been absolutely free of self-importance and vanity. But for the deep-seated arrogance of soul that we call intellectual pride, perhaps there was no better contender than Thomas, the doubting Apostle. Oblivious of the many predictions Jesus had made regarding his resurrection and scoffing at the testimony of ten eye-witnesses, Thomas stubbornly stood his ground and refused to assent to the Lord's revivification. Jesus in turn not only let the man off with a gentle chiding, he also acceded to the skeptic's wishes and actually pulled the disciple's finger and hand into the wound-marks to establish a faith that would withstand martyrdom. If we may construe greed to imply simply a great ambition for acquiring this world's wealth, friend Zacchaeus evidently was a greedy mortal. In all likelihood, after Jesus had sojourned with the enterprising midget and converted the whole well-heeled household, Zacchaeus doubled his already generous contributions to charity. Although the other Mary was in more than one sense a shady lady and not perfectly identifiable, it is she, whoever she is, who qualifies as the representative of lust, having loved not wisely but too well. Her chastened ardor made her the first Christian contemplative. Saul of Tarsus, a posthumous friend of Jesus, was the soul of anger—a hot-headed member of the posse breathing threats of slaughter against the disciples of the Lord. His aggressive personality proved tailor-made for his role of pioneer of the Gospel of Peace and the Law of Love. Two Apostles equally qualify as exponents of envy—the brothers James and John. For they were the ones who silenced the lone-wolf exorcist and, at their mother's instigation, jockeyed for the highest thrones in Heaven. Jesus gently set them aright in the first matter and purified their ambition by challenging them to emulate his heroic sufferings. As for gluttony or, in its widest sense, intemperance, none of the Apostles was exactly ascetical as regards creature comforts; they all regularly were preoccupied with food and drink at certain crucial times. But maybe Matthew, who was given to the good life and had a reputation for setting a groaning board, will do for an example of this capital sin. The tireless preacher and author of the first Gospel came to learn that man did not live on bread alone. Finally, there is Peter—Peter who fell asleep thrice in the Garden of Gethsemani and only dreamed of deeds of derring-do for the Master, Peter who talked a big "line" but took his ease by the fire while Jesus was being scourged. His sloth would one day be converted to an unfaltering zeal that would drive him to the other end of the civilized world and to crucifixion upside-down. Jesus was indeed the friend of sinners, but most of them were really saints in the rough.

To fully fathom our Lord's predilection for moral "losers," we must analyze the workings of divine mercy. One of the best object-lessons in divine mercy occurs, one might have guessed, in Saint Luke's humane biography of Jesus: Chapter 7, the latter half of which is devoted to the penitent woman who stole into the house of Simon the Pharisee. There is a critical sentence in the account that has always puzzled the translator. Apart from the English version of the Jerusalem Bible, originally a French translation of the Scriptures, I know of no rendering of that sentence that avoids the obscurity. Traditionally the passage reads, "Wherefore I say to thee, her sins, many as they are, shall be forgiven her, because she has loved much" (Lk. 7:47). If the notion of "loved much" is understood as meaning "shown much penitence" or "shown ardent penance" (and such would be a very loose interpretation), the sentence makes a little sense; but it is hardly an earth-shaking revelation. Without so free a translation the sentence, especially in context, has a ludicrous and almost blasphemous implication: "This woman has loved every Tom, Dick, and Harry, so she will get off lightly." On the other hand, the reading taken from the Jerusalem Bible is both unambiguous and staggering: "Many sins must have been forgiven this woman, for she shows much love." That this is the true meaning of the observation is borne out by the maxim Jesus appends to the episode: "He who is forgiven little, loves little" (Lk. 7:48)—a dictum that delivers quite a comeuppance to a law-abiding, legalistic, self-esteeming Pharisee. Many sins must have been forgiven this woman, for she shows much love; he who is forgiven little, loves little. At first blush, this stance might sound to some like a licensed charter for flinging caution to the winds and painting the town red. Others may see in the passage a substantiation of an age-old heresy, to the effect that innocent people are somehow inhuman, drab, and shallow, while the man or woman of the world is empathetic, interesting, and mature. Both camps of facile interpreters miss the delicate and daring point of Christ's words. The gist of the passage is this: that we all stand beholden to God; that God loves us superabundantly and unconditionally; that God's mercy is simply

Merciful Heavens!

this love confronting our sins; and that the one who has experienced God's mercy has more experiential grounds than the guiltless for reciprocating God's loving mercy with loving gratitude. Or, to put it another way, granting genuine sorrow, even one's serious sins might prove a blessing in disguise, for they can lead to a more profound awareness of God's love and a warmer gratitude for his mercy. Thus, excluding very holy individuals who may have spiritually touched the living God in prayer or contemplation, forgiven sinners stand a better chance of intuiting and responding to the God of revelation than do those mortals who are without offense but familiar only with a remote First Cause or an invisible Taskmaster. Saint Augustine's life provides eloquent testimony to this phenomenon and to the paradoxical value of guilt expressed in the graphic words: "God writes straight with crooked lines—even sins."

The mechanics of mercy bear looking into more closely; after all, reference to the mercy of God is made in Sacred Scripture over five hundred times! Theodicy, the natural science of God, teaches that God exists, that he is the Creator of all things, that he endows all things with ontological goodness and truth and beauty, and that he maintains all things in existence. It can also reason to the personhood of God. But not until the revelations of the Old and New Testament could man see or dare to acknowledge that God has historically entered into a person-to-person, bilateral relationship with his intelligent creatures. Again and again in the Old Testament, God is identified with his fidelity to a contract, a testament, a promise of great things made to his chosen people. In the New Testament that promise is crystallized into a pledge of God's indwelling in the souls of men here below and of the Beatific Vision through everlasting life hereafter; and in the New Testament God is identified with love. Now, on the one hand, almost every reference made in the Old Testament to God's fidelity mentions God's mercy along with it—as well it may, considering the continual infidelity on the part of the chosen people. (See, e.g., 3 Kgs. 8:23; 2 Chr. 6:14; Neh. 1:5 and 9:32, wherein God is called the one "who keeps covenant and mercy.") On the other hand, the God who is love in the New Testament must inevitably be the God who is mercy; for, as we have seen, personal love in confronting sin is transformed to mercy (just as personal love confronting the offended turns to repentance and gratitude). If this scriptural analysis does not underline the intimate connection—no, the relationship of identity—between love and mercy, consider the following deductions from revelation.

Theologians reason that to propound a natural destiny, a human paradise, for man is a purely speculative exercise; for God has actually, and from the very start of the world, programmed man for a supernatural end: namely, to share God's blessed life for all eternity in Heaven. Obviously, no mortal—or angel, for that matter—can merit such a transcendent destiny. God must stoop to lift him. And that stooping is a mercy. If God, moreover, has given men and angels the radical gift, the sanctifying grace, to barter for eternal rewards, he has done so only in view of the redeeming life and death of his divine Son. *All* grace flows from the Cross, and the Cross is clearly an instrument of mercy. All those, too, who refrain from sinning do so in virtue of efficacious actual graces which are likewise the by-product of the merciful Redemption of the Savior. Even the sinless Virgin Mother and the unfallen angels needed the Savior and were subjects of God's mercy. God is love. But from our creatural standpoint that love is mercy. And it is probably the realization of this essential identity between God and love and between love and mercy that underlies mankind's instinctive delight over a story of conversion or that lures the novelist to toy with the notion of the admirable rogue set off against the flinthearted Pharisee.

Merciful Heavens!

If God is mercy, the corollary is inescapable: man becomes like God by being merciful. Ultimately, the thermometer of a person's goodness is not any number of other moral standards such as self-fulfillment, self-knowledge, self-mastery, devotion to duty, or hewing to some code. Ultimately (and this is a truism of Christianity) it is love of neighbor. But the "hot point" of that love—in man's sub-lunar existence, at least—will be pardoning love, that is, mercy. In the final analysis, granting the radical grace God gives us in his mercy, we will all grow like to God and thereby deserve to dwell with him forever when and only when we forgive each other from our heart: "Do not judge, and you shall not be judged; do not condemn, and you shall not be condemned. Forgive, and you shall be forgiven" (Lk. 6:37). If a man knows God only in the Almighty's manifestations of power and justice, he does not know God. To know God as he truly is requires that one be recipient or at least spectator of his mercy. To see the face of God is to see his mercy: "The Lord show his face to thee and have mercy on thee" (Nm. 6:25). And men become like the God of revelation not so much by the exercise of their power and justice as by their practice of mercy:

> *But mercy is above this sceptred sway;*
> *It is enthroned in the hearts of kings;*
> *It is an attribute of God himself;*
> *And earthly power doth then show likest God's*
> *When mercy seasons justice.*
>
> *(The Merchant of Venice,*
> *IV.i.193-96)*

Lines for a Requiem Card

When Lazarus died God said he slept,
But how He sighed and even wept.
So we can see in tears God shed
How even we should mourn the dead.

Though Mary knew her Son would rise,
At Calvary's view tears filled her eyes.
Though we believe the dead live on,
With her we grieve to see them gone.

The Christian knows no hopeless grief
Like that of those without belief,
But with Christ and Mary I'll condole
Your loss and share your grief of soul.

5. *Putting Faith into Focus*

THROUGHOUT CHRISTIANITY'S history many an individual has survived or succumbed to a personal crisis of faith. But today the crisis looks epidemic, and the *institution* seems to be shaken to its foundations. When times are critical, it is time for a critique. When issues grow crucial, we should get down to the crux of the matter. If wise men head for the cellar in a tornado, we religious must return to the basics of belief during today's theological turbulence. In this month's conference I propose to uncover and underscore what I consider the elemental facets of our faith. The result of my efforts will be a rough, skeleton outline, if you will, of what a Christian's creed is all about. Like all rough things my analysis will probably be ragged, but I hope it proves rugged as well. And if my approach to orthodoxy seems a bit unorthodox and, like a skeleton, weird, I can only counter that a little dose of the fantastic is the best remedy for that familiarity which breeds oblivion as well as contempt. A fresh and fundamental look at the subject reveals three paradoxical features of Christian faith: faith is an encounter but one that exacts surrender; it implies confidence but along with precaution; and it seeks out the transcendent but only in the ordinary. (These headings hardly sound exciting or even enlightening, but they are the most accurate generalizations I could come up with.) Let us explore these paradoxes in an attempt to put our faith into focus and batten down our belief.

If some anthropoid from the Dog Star constellation were

to collar a Christian and ask him what he believed, he would be barking up the wrong tree. It might be appropriate to ask a theosophist to air his airy tenets or to have a Hindu disclose his labyrinth of doctrines or to prod a Mohammedan into confessing the simple and healthy creed embodied in his Koran. But the only telling question to pose to a Christian is not "What?" but "Whom do you believe?"

Obviously, Jesus reiterated divine truths from the Old Testament and revealed new data about the supernatural. But real faith is more than acknowledging and assenting to these truths; it is first and foremost meeting and receiving the person called Jesus. For Jesus was more of a toucher than a teacher, more of a redeemer than a reformer: "The Son of Man has come to serve, and to give his life as a ransom for many" (Mk. 10:45). If Jesus were essentially just a prophet delivering doctrines, his words are disappointingly brief: you could copy out his utterances from a red-letter edition of St. Mark's Gospel onto about ten sheets of notebook paper. Explicit revelations concerning the spiritual universe and the afterlife are few and figurative, most of them merely refinements of Old Testament theology. If Jesus were principally a reformer, his ethical exhortations, though richly suggestive, are exasperatingly meager in detail, especially in the light of what were ultimately to become burning moral issues such as racism, war, marital discord, birth control, usury, crime and punishment, drug abuse, clerical celibacy, and environmental pollution. The primary concern of his three public years and his three empassioned hours was to show us that he was a divine person who loved humanity to death. After they had undergone their freshman year in the Apostolic College, the final exam question Jesus posed to the Twelve was not, "How is Original Sin transmitted?" or even "Which is the greatest of the Commandments?" but, "Who do you say that I am?" The Samaritan woman did not run into town shouting doctrines about efficacious grace or counsels on where to

Putting Faith into Focus 37

worship: she did spread the faith, though, by yelling, "Come and *see a man* who has told me all that I have ever done" (Jn. 4:29). Even when Jesus was professedly engaged in teaching, as when he commented upon the Scriptures in the synagogue, what really made the congregation sit up and take notice, evidently, was not his sublimation of the Law and the Prophets but his personal projection: "He taught them as one who has authority, and not as a scribe" (Mk. 1:22). The Master once and for all laid to rest the idea that faith is simply an intellectual nod to a theological notion when he raised Lazarus from the dead. His short but sweet debate with Martha before her brother was resurrected (Jn. 11:21-27) offers a marvelous insight into the uniquely personal character of Christian faith. Like a well trained Sabbath-School student, Martha had recited—and with conviction—an important tenet of her Jewish faith: "I know that he will rise at the resurrection, on the last day." But Jesus hastened to correct her: "I am the resurrection and the life; he who believes in me, even if he die, shall live; and whoever lives and believes in me shall never die. Do you believe this?" Instantly Martha became aware of this deeper dimension of faith; for instead of answering, "Yes, I'll assent to this new flourish to our eschatalogical doctrine," she blurted out, "Yes, Lord, I believe that you are the Christ, the Son of God, who has come into the world."

To concede that what Jesus declared about the things of God is true is important, but only secondarily; and to do so, supernaturally speaking, is possible only after one discovers that Jesus is the truth: "I am the way and the truth and the life" (Jn. 14:6). Now, some may object that all this talk about faith being an encounter with the person of Jesus is understandable as applied to his contemporaries but that we who are removed thousands of miles and years from the historical Christ have small occasion to bump into the object of our profession. Yet is it not possible, even on a natural level, to know someone well from afar? Most hero-worshippers would protest that they are intimately acquainted with their favorite though an actual encounter with him might give them heart-failure. One need not read many of the recorded words and deeds of the Savior to catch the core of his character. Furthermore, if you look closely at the definition of faith sculptured by the Fathers of the First Vatican Council—a definition that is not so cold and impersonal in the final analysis—you will see that anyone can come into a certain ontological contact with Jesus. They taught that faith is "a supernatural virtue whereby, with *God inspiring* and *grace helping*, we give assent to truths revealed by him . . . who can neither deceive nor be deceived." Jesus is alive and well, and sends his love in the form of illuminating and enlivening graces through the Holy Spirit: "But when the Advocate has come, the Spirit of truth who proceeds from the Father, he will bear witness concerning me . . . And when he, the Spirit of truth, has come, he will teach you all the truth . . . he will glorify me because he will receive of what is mine and declare it to you" (Jn. 15:26; 16:13-14).

Through the agency of the Holy Spirit, the twentieth-century believer can advance from encounter to acquaintance to fast friendship with Jesus by the inner dialogue of prayer and meditation. So what does it matter if another authentic Gospel (like certain Epistles of St. Paul's) had been written but was lost? What does it matter if the Master's words were scanty, cumbered with Aramaic idioms, or conditioned by long-ago events in an inconsequential oriental country? To the believer Jesus is "the same yesterday, today, yes, and forever": a God-man whom prayer and grace render closer than one's spouse or alter ego. If I have dwelt long on this first facet of faith, it is because it is the most central, the most crucial, especially in these days of doctrinal crisis.

"Encounter" is a good word to designate this primary facet of faith since its first dictionary meaning is "to meet

Putting Faith into Focus

unexpectedly"; but since nobody can meet Jesus in faith and remain unchanged, "encounter" is just the right word, for its second dictionary meaning is "to meet in battle." To know Jesus, as opposed to knowing about him, is to fall beneath his spell, to be enthralled by him and made his vassal. Jesus demands nothing less than surrender. To put it more graphically, the Lord does not simply ask of you, as would any mere moralist or reformer, that you run your life more on the straight and narrow; he bids you to put him in the driver's seat.

If you were to flip through the pages of the Synoptics, you would receive the distinct impression that Jesus "flipped" over just one situation—that is, that over this one situation his heartbeat quickened, his face flushed with joy, his life seemed worthwhile. And that was encountering a person at his wits' end, a desperate soul who seemed to have gravitated to the Master as a last resort. Think of the man whose epileptic youngster kept throwing himself into the fireplace every time his parents turned their back; the sinful woman who slinked into Simon's supper and gave Jesus' feet a rub-down with her lovely tresses; the blind men on the way to Jericho who practically burst their lungs shouting for the itinerant preacher to touch them; the Centurion, Jairus, the hemorrhaging woman, the importunate Samaritan lady. Their number is legion: the whole crowd of first-generation converts to Christianity, it would seem, were people in dire need, people with problems, people who were desperate. Jesus rejoiced to meet such as these because they were disposed to surrender themselves to his all-pervasive influence. And throughout the annals of Christendom the seed of faith has taken fastest root amid the debris of personal failure and watered with the tears of a crying need. Francis Thompson, for example, remembering the days when as a penniless drug-addict he slept under newspapers in Hyde Park, poetically recorded the formula for faith:

But when so sad, thou canst not sadder,
Cry, and upon thy so-sore loss,
Shall shine the traffic of Jacob's ladder
Pitched betwixt Heaven and Charing Cross.

Yea, in the night, my soul, my daughter,
Cry, clinging Heaven by the hems.
And lo! Christ walking on the water,
Not of Gennesareth but Thames.

Many who admire Jesus but have not come to him with their own resources for coping with life exhausted have never gone "all the way" and have thus far only signed a truce with Christ the King. One of three obstacles may be blocking the way to the surrender implicit in genuine faith. The first and commonest is the fear that they will get hurt. Their reserved faith is like that of the Prince of Wales in the following episode. Back at the turn of the century, when George V of England was the Prince of Wales, he paid a visit to Canada while a famous French aerialist was performing there. When the Prince heard the highwire artist claim that he could push a wheelbarrow across the Canadian Falls, he registered disbelief. But true to his boast, the Frenchman succeeded in inching the conveyance to the farther bank, where the Prince looked on in amazement. "Now do you believe me?" queried the performer. "Quite!" replied the dignitary. "Then get into the wheelbarrow, and I'll push you back to the other side," challenged the aerialist. "But I don't believe you that much!" was the Prince's reply. So say many of the "faithful" to Jesus who would direct their lives.

Others "of little faith" feel squeamish about depending on another person so thoroughly. Imbued with the Western, particularly the Emersonian-American, attitude of self-reliance, they consider such wholehearted commitment as servile and pusillanimous or as foolish as infatuation. Their

Putting Faith into Focus 41

motto is, "I'd rather do it myself!" They do not yet understand the Scriptures which say, "My ways are not your ways." Still others with wavering faith regard themselves as too unworthy to invite the Lord all the way into their life and are more inclined to echo the response of the sweaty, swearing, swaggering trawler, "Sir, depart from me, for I am a sinful man." These forget that one trysts with Jesus on a come-as-you-are basis. As the Jesuit spiritual writer Fr. Bernard Basset demonstrates with copious quotes, the Lord constantly, almost embarrassingly, addressed the "heart" of his hearers and virtually closed every public sermon with the words, "Son, give me your heart." And the "heart" is the person at his core, not the ideal ego, not the public image one projects, not even the shifting construct of what one thinks he is, for better or for worse—but the pock-marked, piebald, gap-toothed soul that each of us really is. This is what Jesus wants, what he can work with. It is this heart-of-heart tenement (with its basement and attic, slop-closets and suites) that Jesus desires to inhabit. Jesus, remember, grew really excited when he came across a self-confessed moral "slob"; for he forthwith laid hold of Peter: "Come follow me, and I will make you a fisher of men." These three obstacles—fear, self-reliance, and self-disgust—once removed, the encounter of faith can become a surrender for life.

The second feature of genuine faith, I say, is confidence and caution, but not in the sense of the words you probably assume I intend. For I do not mean to imply that the Christian's hope and optimism are qualified, conditional, or hedged. No, there are no *confer* footnotes in the Book called Good or retractions appendixed to the biography entitled The Good News. I will explain just what I mean by "caution" shortly, after enlarging on the categorical confidence that faith entails.

If our anthropoid from the Dog Star constellation were to scan the Gospels for the first time, he would probably react to them like a typical earthling, like, say, a Pharisee: "This Good News is too good to be true." Such a reaction would be entirely human, reasonable, and realistic—but wrong. The Gospels not only promise but applaud great expectations on the part of believers, individually and corporately. And even if you were not a believer but simply a philosopher who had reasoned to God's existence and labeled him "The Other," as philosophers have, might you not conclude that God's management of the future, your own and the world's, would unspeakably transcend human hopes? In the face of successive acts of the human tragedy that is history, in the knowledge of innumerable acts of self-disappointment, in the worldwide atmosphere of "business as usual," in the cold light of worldy wisdom that counsels survival of the fittest and the *quid-pro-quo* mentality, it is all but impossible to take a person like Jesus, with a pocketful of miracles at his word. It is much easier to subscribe to the beatitude the Master did not coin "Blessed are those who expect nothing, for they shall not be disappointed." Before advancing in faith, we must all recognize and vigorously shake off this earthbound attitude. Perhaps the man of the following anecdote is a caricature; even so, there is a bit of him in each of us.

A fellow was out driving one Sunday evening, when his rear tire blew out. He reached into the glove compartment for his flashlight but mused, "Oh, I forgot—Johnny took it on his camping trip." After lifting the spare tire from his trunk, he felt around for his auto jack—but to no avail. "Son of a gun," he thought, "I lent it to Jones Saturday morning." It seemed to him he was in the middle of nowhere, but as he strolled a short way up the hill, he spied a farmhouse nearby. "Dollars to doughnuts, they don't own a jack," he mumbled under his breath. But catching a glimpse of a fender on the further side of the house, he reasoned, "They'll probably charge this city-slicker a five-spot to rent the thing." By the

Putting Faith into Focus

time he reached the entrance walk, the house lights went out. "They'll be dead to the world in seconds," he thought. Finding no bell, he rapped on the door, little hoping to rouse the occupants from their second-story bedrooms. A nightcapped oldster leaned out from a second-floor window and called down, "Who is it?" "You can keep your galdarned jack!" shouted our hero, and he stomped off in disgust.

His outlook on life painfully lacked the uplook Jesus took great pains to inculcate. Permit me to paraphrase here Luke 11:11-13, to bring home the point. Jesus very likely was addressing dock-workers and fishermen near Lake Gennesareth and said to them: "If your kids ask you for a bun, do you give them a boulder? If they beg you for an egg, what do you do, hand them a scorpion? When they reach for a sardine, do you pass them a snake? Of course you don't. And if you, who are really nothing but a bunch of bozos, at least know how to give your kids a treat, don't you think that your Father in Heaven is going to give you the best gift you ever got in your life, the Good Spirit?" Just listen to the promises: rewards in good measure, shaken down (unlike a bag of potato chips), and brimming over; phenomenal growth that starts as small as a mustard seed which a sparrow could gobble up a dozen at a time and issues in a bush big enough for a flock to nest in; a new life not only initiated but also nurtured to abundant perfection by the Almighty's hand; all other things than God that you need—suits, hamburger, fuel—thrown into the bargain; dreams and visions whispered into your mind by the Holy Spirit who never speaks in jest; an indwelling voice of God that prays to God in your every good intention with unutterable groanings; bodies that will eventually shine like stars; citizenship in a bejeweled metropolis where every tear will be dried and every sigh assuaged; good things, in short, that no mortal eye has ever beheld or human ear has ever heard.

The point though is, do we, in spite of temporal appearances, believe it all? Do we habitually behave as if we were heirs to a fortune, winners of a sweepstake, recipients of a windfall—children of God? Saint Francis of Assisi did. It is reported that his fellow friars could send him into an ecstasy almost at will just by whispering the word "Heaven" to the man. Prescinding from congenital sad dispositions or transitory bouts with the blues, and occasional moral abberrations, there is something radically amiss with the faith of that Christian who regards life pessimistically, glumly, negatively, cynically, skeptically, even realistically; for such an attitude belies the Good News.

Genuine faith is unconditionally confident, is sure; but it is not cocksure. It comes with no strings attached, but it is not all sewed up. A twofold precaution is called for: openness of soul so that God can work his will in us, and open-mindedness so that we can acknowledge his work in the souls of others.

A bird's eye view of Old Testament history reveals a certain dialectic of God's dealings with his Chosen People. At times he had to bring in his sheep lest they jump the fence and land amid the encircling polytheism. At others he was obliged to scatter the sheep inasmuch as they had turned tail to the Shepherd and gazed fixedly at one another in catatonic complacency. The constant threat to monotheism was simple and discernible; the periodic peril of institutionalism was subtle and insidious. The former may have misled the Israelites into worshipping strange gods; the latter certainly tended to replace worship with patriotism and the divinity with ritual. Whenever the Chosen People grew satisfied that they had adequately placated Yahweh and could get on with more serious matters, Yahweh pulled the rug from beneath them, usually in the form of a degrading exile. The institutional Christian faces a similar hazard. He can hide behind his neat creed, code, and cult from the living God and can rationalize away the intrusive promptings of the

Putting Faith into Focus

Holy Spirit. He can contribute to St. Peter's Pence and ignore a sick aunt. He can come to fisticuffs in defense of the Mass and secularize his Sunday. He can recite the Lord's Prayer daily and throw a fit over his wife's car accident. But the man of faith is more imaginative and more flexible than that. He scrutinizes all misfortunes, from a coronary thrombosis to a pimple on the nose, and asks, "What is it God means by this visitation of his Providence?" He prays over his financial predicaments. Like Tobias he foregoes his supper occasionally to bury the dead—or a grudge. He cracks the family Bible with regularity, knowing that "all Scripture is inspired by God and useful for teaching, for reproving, for correcting, for instructing in justice" (2 Tm. 3:16). He is not greatly upset when his plans are upset. He moves on to another vocation if prayer and Providence so dictate as expeditely as Saint Paul or Saint Francis shook the dust from their feet outside of fruitless mission fields. He makes a vigil, a retreat, a donation when some problem persistently bedevils him. He is alert to see the Lord's lesser brethren in drunks and drop-outs, in the helpless and the hopeless. In brief, he is, as far as his sanity will foreseeably allow, available to the Master. And his watchword is, "Speak, Lord, your servant hears." If God is to work miracles in our lives, we must not bind his hands or deny the ongoing dynamics of his providence and inspiration.

We must also cultivate open-mindedness in regard to the spirituality, though not the creed, of those outside the Church. Jesus and Saint Paul not only tolerated people of other persuasions, they also toasted every evidence of the Holy Spirit in them. When John boasted to Jesus that he had tried to stifle a non-Christian who was exorcising in the neighborhood, Jesus put down the "beloved" disciple thus: "Do not forbid him . . . for he who is not against you is for you." Jesus also reminded his followers that the "other sheep" not of the fold are, nevertheless, "his sheep." Saint Paul's finger-pointing apology for the Jews in Romans 11 and powerful appeal for forbearance towards those with partial faith in Romans 14 are too lengthy to analyze here; but these passages are a sure cure for triumphalism. In this connection, I cannot help mentioning Saint Paul's treatment of the Athenians. To savor the episode fully, we must realize that Paul was anything but a flaming liberal or addle-headed relativist about the faith and that the then-present populace of Athens were philosophical dilettantes and notoriously unspiritual. Paul started his sermon with a joke about their scrupulous polytheism which, if it was no compliment to their religious sensitivity, was one to their sense of humor. Then he condescended to quote a Greek poet of their acquaintance and went so far as to concede to them—many of them dirty, old men—that God was not far off from any one of them. Surely, then, the faithful must be alert not to break the reed of another's crooked faith or to blow out the smoldering spark of spirituality in those outside the Church.

The third paradoxical feature of faith is that it seeks out the transcendental but only in the ordinary. It may be belaboring the obvious (as one tends to do in emphasizing basics), but the object of faith is invisible reality, that is, God and his grace, the soul and its immortal destiny: "Our hearts, O Lord, were made for thee and shall not rest until they rest in thee," Saint Augustine put it. Essentially, faith has nothing to do with many other noble values and constructive enterprises that terminate in man and on earth, such as public welfare, mental and physical health, or art and science. But, oddly enough, these uplifting endeavors, if they are not easily substituted for the supernatural, are often made the measuring stick for the relevancy of religion. And so to put the believer at his ease on this score, I want to shed some scriptural light on these temporal matters.

If Jesus Christ were the superstar of the indigent masses, he certainly passed up golden opportunities to shine in their eyes. Precisely when the poor and hungry thought they had

Putting Faith into Focus

found a likely candidate for a king who would dole out bread and sermons, Jesus slipped behind the curtains. He repeatedly cautioned the populace about the snare of brimming barns, sumptuous feasts, and soft garments. He spoke of gaining a world and losing a soul. He cured the sick, but not all of them, nor at one, fell swoop. His miracles were chaste and economical: all were calculated primarily to win faith in his divinity and entry to the soul. He deftly evaded political commentary by telling the Roman soldiers merely to refrain from plundering, making false accusations, and grumbling over their pay and by counselling the citizenry simply to pay their taxes and do their civic duty. He was little impressed with pageantry, found theological hair-splitting otiose, and exposed the arrogance and hypocrisy behind ceremonial decorum and upper-class etiquette. His interest, in short, were in the world but not of it.

Saint Paul, too, was not exactly afire to clear the slums, recommend diets, demolish depression, write plays, or further philosophy. His digression on charity in the first Epistle to the Corinthians should be studied for more than its eloqiemce; For in it, he makes an unsettling revelation which forever distinguishes supernatural concern from even the most sacrificial altruism: "And if I distribute all my goods to feed the poor, and if I deliver my body to be burned yet do not have charity, it profits me nothing" (1 Cor. 13:3). The tentmaker from Tarsus was hardly a hermit or Puritan in regard to the civilized world; but still he knew in his bones that the Crucified Christ he preached would always be a scandal to the politically ambitious and a stumbling block to sophisticates.

Health, welfare, and culture are not inconsequential affairs; but they are in the world and of it. This is not to say that they do not impinge upon religion. We live in an age of unprecedented problems, many of which we have a serious moral duty to address. The obligation rises variously: from the dictates of justice and charity to the demands of talents and destiny. Our society is neurotic and by turns paranoid and schizophrenic: hence the need for therapeutic personalism. Racial, economic, and environmental imbalances call for active involvement. Knowledge explosions and culture-shocks call for scientists and poets to harness and harmonize. However, none of these endeavors should be allowed to overshadow or encroach upon the pursuit of the supernatural, much less replace it. Not on bread or brotherhood, books or beauty alone does man live.

Though faith tells us to find the transcendent God, it also directs us to find him in our own backyard. In his day Jesus moved between roughly two religious factions—the Pharisees and the Sadducees. The former were traditionalists who divinized the past; the latter, liberals who either toyed with the latest spiritual fad or anticipated a new and shining Zion. For both camps his words must have fallen like a bombshell: "The Kingdom of God is in your midst." This is to say, the will of God and our sanctification lie not in the miracle-studded past or spectacular future, but under our nose. By his every parable and prayer, his every sacrament and statute, Jesus apotheosized the near and the now, the common and the commonplace. His prophecies may have been couched in typically cosmic language, but his asceticism at all levels might be aptly labelled "Holiness in the Humdrum." Proximity to God, he measured in terms of a cup of cold water, a closeted prayer, a widow's mite, a visit to the sick, a lent cloak, a beggar's dole, a grace at table, an edified child, a leper's gratitude, a daily cross, and a memorial supper. Not only to the woman at the well, but to every believer and wherever he is "at," Jesus whispers: "If thou didst know the gift of God . . ."

To quest for God and the will of God elsewhere than under one's nose is to follow, at best, a disappointing and, at worst, a pernicious will-o'-the-wisp. Dabbling in the occult, the bizarre, the novel, and the sensational may be a harmless pastime. But all too many sophisticated and independent spirits have squandered heart and mind and body in the serious but futile hope of experiencing God in the extraordinary. They have pinned their faith on exotic trinities like LSD or ESP or UFO. They look for epiphanies in Zen, astrology, yoga, necromancy. They reach for preternatural powers in witchcraft, demon-worship, psychocybernetics. To all of these anxious searchers, God shouts, "Be still, and know that I am God." But I would address a word of warning, too, to my fellow faithful who habitually hanker after the sensational and experimental in religion—with their soup-kitchens and soap-boxes, their sensitivity retreats and leavened Mass-bread, their chain novenas and bleeding statues: "Thou art busy about many things; one thing is necessary."

This, then, concludes my efforts at putting faith into focus. It should be obvious by now that I in no way attempted to outline or explain the articles of the Creed. My objective was simply to clear the air in regard to the general atmosphere of Christian faith, since I thought it did need clearing. Faith is *the* important virtue, and all nature conspires to teach its primacy. As Father John Bannister Tabb reflected during one night of insomnia while awaiting the dawn:

> *In every seed, to breathe the flower,*
> *In every drop of dew—*
> *To reverence the cloistered star*
> *Within the distant blue;*
>
> *To await the promise of the bow*
> *Despite the cloud between—*
> *Is faith, the fervid evidence*
> *Of loveliness unseen.*

Grow Old Along with Me

Falling hair and darkening tooth,
Wrinkles wrought on the face of youth,
Shall you give me cause for ruth?
Ha! you tell but half the truth.

Mar my features as you may,
The hidden growth you but betray:
Dimpled graces day by day
God ferments in this jar of clay.

Ruin the course of time betrays.
And growth requires a run of days.
Wine gets tang in a crumbling vase;
The inner man thrives while the outer decays.

6. *Hounds of Heaven*

A SHORT WHILE back I had occasion to visit our onetime Franciscan novitiate in Lafayette, New Jersey. There I sauntered into the library and ran my eye over the somewhat nondescript collection: a piebald assortment composed of the venerable leavings of the old Paterson novitiate library, donations of second copies from sundry monasteries in the Province, and a fair number of bright new-theology volumes. Abstractedly I pulled down a stout book with a purple cover layered with a fuzz of dust and riffled its glossy pages. The work was a labor of love by some Benedictine of the 'forties. About five hundred pages long, it presented a photograph and detailed biography of nearly two hundred famous Catholic authors of the day: a roster as prestigious as it was prodigious. For the next three hours I was lost in amazement over the thing. As I browsed through the text, long-dormant emotions of sectarian pride and confidence—I blush to say—surged in my breast. At least half of the writers in question were converts to the Church—world-famous, cerebral souls who had entered the Faith at the height of their successful and sophisticated lives.

It was then that I recalled a twenty-year-old scene from my past. But the vision appeared so alien and remote in view of the Church's present depression, eclipse, turbulence, or call it what you will, that the reverie seemed a century old. I allude to the scene of Boston College bookstore circa 1950: the shelves bulging with publications by Sheed & Ward, Herder & Herder, Bruce, and dozens of other Catholic book firms; the walls plastered with blow-ups of Hilaire Belloc,

G. K. Chesterton, Leon Bloy, Graham Greene, Evelyn Waugh, Caryll Houselander, Arnold Lunn, Alfred Noyes, and scads of other Catholic authors, most of whom were converts. My apostolic zeal—so constant and fervent then, so precarious and lukewarm lately—began to rekindle. Resisting the temptation to purloin the purple relic in my hands, I replaced it on the bookshelf. But I had resolved to keep aglow this reborn zeal for the apostolate and to write something to reawaken ecclesiastical esteem and missionary enthusiasm for my coreligionists.

To give this conference some transparent shape, let me say that I propose to discuss conversion to the Faith under three headings. First, I want to show that convert-making is still a going concern in the twentieth century (including the post-Vatican II era). Next, I hope to sell the reader on two important reasons for selling the Faith. Finally, I will suggest various ways of winning converts that have proved effective for myself and others of my acquaintance. My object in this conference is to enlist more, and more eager, hounds of Heaven. That is, I am trying to fetch sheepdogs for the Good Shepherd to help the Lord round up many of his sheep that are not (yet) of his Fold.

Let me confess at the outset, the last ten years have hardly been the Church's Second Spring, in the English-speaking world at least. The novitiate I mentioned earlier, built to house ninety novices, was closed a few years ago for lack of vocations. Today, for many people, Catholic as well as non-, the Pope has become identified as public enemy number one. Hosts of ecclesiastical skeletons-in-the-closet have been paraded before the public; front-bench theologians and even Cardinals have literally wrangled over bedrock matters of orthodoxy. (Secular no less than spiritual factors of mind-staggering complexity are no doubt responsible for the upheavals of the 'sixties and the rampant confusion in the ranks of the Church Militant). Little wonder, then, that the

Hounds of Heaven

twentieth century may not go down in Church history as the heyday of convert-making.

Nevertheless, converts are still being made, made in remarkable numbers, made among remarkable people. According to the *1971 Catholic Almanac* nearly ninety-three thousand people in the United States had entered the Church the previous year, despite the Pope's unpopularity, unprecedented defection from the clergy and religious life, and well publicized infighting among theologians. The past decade, moreover, has seen the conversion of some nationally famous people of high repute with nothing earthly to gain from the move. The year before he died Gary Cooper came into the Church and found the sacraments an undeniable help in playing his last role—the strong, silent type—as a victim of terminal cancer. Within the last few years, Hank Aaron, outfielder for the Milwaukee Braves, and Brooks Robinson, Baltimore third baseman, became Catholics. Perhaps they were just following the lead of two other athletes converted earlier in the century, Knute Rockne and Babe Ruth. A few years back Kate Smith, edified by the good life and pious death of her manager, Ted Collins, entered the Church. England's all-time best comedy-tragedy actor, Sir Alec Guinness, also was received into the Catholic Church within recent years. Lucy B. (Johnson) Nugent's conversion made headlines in the late 'sixties; but I venture to say that many another personage has entered the Church in these latter days without front-page notice. It is devilishly difficult to find lists of recent well-known converts; for the Catholic press, inspired by the Scripture which says, "Put not your trust in princes," usually refrains from broadcasting converts to the Faith until they are safely buried with benefit of the Last Rites.

Restricting my survey still to the twentieth century, I would now like to gesture to the outstanding converts who entered the Church before the 'sixties. Those years, after all, which embraced two world wars and were filled with the atmosphere of sophisticated materialism and sanguine scientism, were hardly more conducive to Romish conversion than the disturbing 'sixties. Besides, many of these dignitaries are living, and living still secure within the arms of Holy Mother Church. A very cursory bit of research has revealed to me the following well-known Catholic converts.

To begin, there is a clutch of distinguished Englishmen: G. K. Chesterton, Christopher Dawson, Eric Gill, Douglas Hyde, Arnold Lunn, Bruce Marshall, Alfred Noyes, Graham Greene, and Evelyn Waugh. A number of famous men converts became priests, such as Robert Hugh Benson, Owen Dudley (of Masterful Monk fame), Msgr. Ronald Knox, Thomas Merton, and Bernard Hubbard, Jesuit explorer. Famous women converts include Sigrid Undset (Nobel awardist), Gertrude von le Fort, Gretta Palmer, Dame Edith Sitwell, Ambassador Clare Boothe Luce, Sheila Kaye-Smith, Marion Taggart, Rosalind Murray (wife of Arnold Toynbee), and Frances Parkingson Keyes. Among famous Jewish converts are composer Gustav Mahler, conductor Otto Klemperer, apologist Arthur Goldstein, Met baritone Leonard Warren, musician Wanda Landowska, author Maurice Baring, educator Waldemar Gurian, writer Karl Stern, journalist Max Fisher, and priest-psychologist Raphael Simon—not to mention Franz Werfel and Henri Bergson, both of whom confessed to moral adhesion to the Catholic Church. (Family considerations alone kept them from officially embracing the Faith.) A quick scan of the world at large turns up the following list of important converts: Educator John Wu, prime-minister (Japan, 1946-1954) Shigeru Yoshida, Admiral Yamamoto, author Johannes Jorgensen, priest-psychologist Ignace Lepp, philosophers Jacques Maritain and Gabriel Marcel, artist Geroge Roualt, and writers Giovanni Papini and Sven Stolpe—not to mention born Catholics who rediscovered their Faith, like Charles de Foucauld and Alexis Carrel.

Figures who loom large in American history are Buffalo Bill Cody, Joel Chandler Harris (Uncle Remus), Charles and John Stoddard, Theodore Maynard, as well as the following disparate list of men: poet Joyce Kilmer, author Fulton Oursler, Justice Sherman Minton, Senator Robert Wagner, Governor Nathan Miller, editor George Nathan, historian Carleton Hayes, organist R. K. Biggs, CARE official Geoffrey Baldwin, journalist Heywood Broun, Russian ambassador William Bullit, and ex-Communist writers Claude McKay and Louis Budenz. In view of this striking list of Catholic converts, the Church may readily sigh with relief, "We must be doing something right," regardless of all the contemporary self-scrutiny and the chest-beating that only yesterday replaced the chest-thumping and apostolic militancy.

Space does not permit me to explain the phenomenon in detail; but in the case of every one of the aforementioned dignitaries, some human being was instrumental in the conversion—some Catholic, from a layman to a bishop, functioned, so to speak, as a middleman. It follows that you and I could play a similar role in the making of still another convert. But human nature—even regenerate human nature—being what it is, most of the Faithful are inclined to rest content with "keeping the Faith" in smug security and snug complacency rather than exerting themselves to spread that Faith. So it is not exactly idle to pose and answer the question: Why should one want to sell the Faith to an "outsider"—why should one go poking his sectarian nose into other people's spiritual business? Two answers suggest themselves: God commands us to sell the Faith; and the Faith—even in the befuddled 'seventies—is an eminently salable commodity. Therefore, before we turn our attention to the customer and ways of attracting him into the supernatural market, it behooves us to scrutinize our Executive's memo and to familiarize ourselves with the selling points of the product.

Frankly speaking, I was rather disappointed when I searched the New Testament for texts that clearly exhorted the Faithful to spread the Faith. The Gospels furnished none; and the Epistles, just a few. But, on second thought, I realized that there was good reason for such a paucity of explicit exhortations and that a general missionary injunction was clearly and constantly implied in the whole of the New Testament. Although there are any number of Gospel passages that enjoin the Apostles to preach the Word and baptize all and sundry, the ordinary member of the Church is given no similar command to carry the Good News in this section of the New Testament because not until after the Ascension was the Church truly established or the Good News actually completed. As for the Epistles, most of them were occasioned by, and addressed to, some particular problem that had arisen in a recently converted territory; and these problems almost invariably required that the Apostles (Paul, Peter, James, John, and Jude) simply urge their neophytes to keep (and live) the Faith that had been entrusted to them. (On re-reading these Epistles, I was once more impressed with the precarious state of the early Church and the onslaughts of ambient heresy: the Church's difficulties today pale by comparison.)

The universal obligation to sell the Faith, however, is manifest from the whole tenor of the Epistles and from a few emphatic exhortations. That all members of the Church share the duty of sharing the Faith is heavily implied from four distinct considerations, which I may touch on briefly without citing any one scriptural passage. First, it is obvious that belief and salvation and sanctification are, in the Christian dispensation (as they were in the Old Testament economy of grace) preeminently social in implication, not merely private and personal. One's faith came through hearing another preach, and one was baptized into a visible society, the Ecclesia (Greek for Assembly) or Church. The

Hounds of Heaven 57

Christian's vocation, then, is communal: other-oriented in origin and in fulfillment. All Christians must reach out to help make firm and swell the community of believers, working as well as praying that God's kingdom come. The message carried to heroic lengths by the first Apostles and their appointed disciples was the Gospel. *Gospel*, as you are probably well aware, means "Good News"; it is of the nature of all news, favorable or unfavorable, to be spread abroad. Every member of the Church is, therefore, obliged to gossip the message in view of the good-tidings character of the Faith. Spreading Christianity, also, devolves on the ordinary Church member as a consequence of charity, the rock-bottom virtue of Christian ethics. If all of Christ's followers are ceaselessly bound to wish others well and to do them good, sharing the Faith and all its concomitant blessings would seem to be the foremost dictate of charity on the part of all Christians. Finally, the Epistles are full of express commands to the Faithful to assist the ambassadors of the Word of God by prayer and monetary sacrifice; all the more, then, ought they to help the apostolate by imitation as far as their talents and opportunities allow.

To see God's explicit summons of all Christians to sell the Faith, let us turn now to specific passages in Sacred Scripture. Saint Paul, to begin with, lays down the principle that God desires every human being to be afforded access to the Faith—which is possible, obviously, only if all Christians cooperate in the apostolate: "This is good and agreeable in the sight of God our Savior; who wishes all men to be saved and *to come to a knowledge of the truth*" (1 Tm. 2:3-4). That God wants all members of the Church to attract others to the Faith by good example is evident from two Pauline Letters: "Do all things without murmuring and without questioning, so as to be blameless and guileless, children of God without blemish in the midst of a depraved and perverse generation" (Phil. 2:15); and, more pointedly, "Walk in wisdom as regards outsiders, making the most of your time. Let your speech, while always attractive, be seasoned with salt, that you may know how you ought to answer each one" (Col. 4:6). It is to the dictum of Saint James that we may trace the notion popular among our Catholic parents to the effect that anyone who makes a convert in life secures his own eternal reward: "My brethren, if any one of you strays from the truth and someone brings him back, he ought to know that he who causes a sinner to be brought back from his misguided way, will save his soul from death, and will cover a multitude of sins" (Jas. 5:19-20). But the real *locus* of Christian doctrine on the lay apostolate is to be found in Saint Peter's wonderful Epistle: "You, however, are a chosen race, a royal priesthood, a holy nation, a purchased people; *that you may proclaim* the perfections of him who has called you out of darkness into his marvelous light . . . . Be ready always with an answer to everyone who asks a reason for the hope that is in you" (1 Pt. 2:9; 3:15). From all of the preceding, then, it is clear what the Boss's orders are: Go and sell the product!

The Faith, truth to tell, is such an attractive package that selling it to ordinary people of good will should be a snap. I can best explain this assertion by drawing upon an example in my own family history. Uncle George, who was married to my mother's kid sister, was the only near relation who was not a Catholic. Though he grew up in a fairly devout Lutheran family, he ceased going to the Lutheran church after marrying Aunt Gert; in fact, he ceased going to any church for a dozen years or so, though he never hindered his wife from practicing her Faith (which she was inclined to do quite ostentatiously), and readily chauffered her and their son to Sunday Mass, reading the Sunday newspaper in the car until Mass "was out." In later years George would attend the Mass with his wife and son at Christmas, Easter, and on an occasional Sunday. About the time my aunt and uncle had celebrated their twenty-fifth wedding anniversary, I was approaching my Ordination. A few weeks before the event, my mother, from out of the blue, wrote me a letter asking me to invite Uncle George to enter the Church. I had a number of qualms about the proposal: for one thing, I had never been very close to this uncle because there had always been some vague ill will or, at least, uneasiness between my father and Uncle George; for another, as far as I could see, George was one darn fine guy, a real Gary Cooper type, whom I thought I would offend by pointing out his spiritual shortcomings. But on a chance inspiration I decided to write Uncle George what proved to be my only letter ever to him and probably the longest epistle I ever penned in my life. I didn't breathe a word about anybody's shortcomings, however; I just simply put to him the case for joining the Catholic Church after assuring him that I thought he was certainly Heaven-bound as things already stood. To recap some of the advantages of life *inside* the Church, as I described them to Uncle George, I started off with what could have proved a questionable blessing: Confession.

What looked like the most ponderous obstacle, I assured him, was really the most palpable advantage. Life holds few heartaches so benumbing and pervasive as the awareness of (or even the suspicion of) unforgiven guilt, whereas a good conscience ever makes the best pillow. For the small pain of examining one's conscience, the slight botheration of slipping into "the Box," and the momentary humiliation of telling one's sins to an anonymous man in the dark, a person could have the weight of a lifetime of guilt, the queasy atmosphere of doubt, the burning burden of cowardice flicked away for good in a trice. (The great G. K. Chesterton was hounded by reporters to reveal the devious reasonings that had led him to embrace an outdated and plebian Persuasion; he answered unabashedly: "To go to Confession.") Next I elaborated for Uncle George the consolations, sometimes even physically perceptible, of receiving our Lord Jesus under the thin veil of the Sacred Species. I told him that I had known moments of peace after consuming Holy Communion that meant more to me than thousands of dollars—a peace no money could buy. And I had found an undeniable strength at the Lord's Table that helped me immensely to cope with "the life of this world." Then I went on to extol participation in the Holy Sacrifice of the Mass, not a prayer one says, but a thing one does that shares in Christ's dynamic Passion and redeems my day and my life from sin, imperfection, insignificance, irrelevance, and tedium. And then there are the answers, the answers! The teaching Church had (and in every eternally important matter, still has) the answers to all the doubts, misgivings, quandaries, and quibbles of the human heart—and she supplies them freely, impartially, calmly, and rationally whenever asked. Neither can she err in positing the answers, nor can her members corporately blunder in grasping them. Next to be considered was the power of the Mystical Body and the invisible network among the Faithful that enables all to mutually benefit from the prayers, good works, and sacrifices of five (now, six) hundred million souls around the globe—this along with secret spiritual communion among all the motley hosts of saints, the heroes and heroines, great and small, in Purgatory and Heaven. At length, I reminded Uncle George of the sweet consolation of the Last Rites—sick bed confession and Holy Viaticum, or all-annealing Extreme Unction and the promise of Rosaries and Masses. Such, briefly, was the honest-to-God bill I tried to sell Uncle George. A week after I was ordained, it was my thrill to celebrate a first Solemn High Mass in my local parish church. When I saw Uncle George kneeling beside Aunt Gert at the Communion rail, I nearly nodded him away. I could hardly believe it, but old Uncle George had bought the package. He was like a kid with a new toy thereafter. He attended daily Mass, received Communion every morning, said the Rosary every night, and went to the novena to the Sorrowful Mother every Friday for the next six years before he died. Believe me, I take very little of the credit for this conversion: it all depended unquestionably upon decades of prayer and good works on the part of his wife and upon the irresistible features of the true Faith. *Non nobis, Domine, non nobis.*

We come at last to the third section of this conference, ways of winning converts. Let it be understood from the start that I eschew all high-pressured approaches and every sensational spiritual pitch (I will forego naming names here of sects that proselytize so incessantly, so blatantly, so obtrusively that they seem driven by masochistic motives). And I eschew such on good grounds. First, Faith is a divine gift which no apostle, however zealous, can bestow: "No one comes to me unless he be called by my Father" (Jn. 6:66); second, it is patently unChristian to harass or bother people: "Strive to live peacefully, minding your own affairs, working with your own hands, as we charged you, so that you may walk becomingly towards outsiders" (1 Thes. 4:11); and third, the sensational and emotional are facile pitfalls for the egocentric soul. Again, by way of preface to the matter at hand, I would like to point out the mechanics underlying all the suggestions for winning converts to be proposed. And that is simply this: we of the household of the Faith, really, have but one thing to do calmly and coolly, in season and out of season—ask people if they are interested in the Catholic Church. For my personal experience and that of many another priest has shown that many, many non-Catholics are just waiting for an invitation to examine the Faith, if not to enter it outright. Every convert-making gimmick only occasions or telegraphs such an invitation. The so-called secret of success in winning converts was demonstrated to me by a wonderfully apostolic schoolmarm I had in the twelfth grade. Once when I was visiting her house and sitting talking to her in the parlor, she heard a footfall at the front door. It was a grizzled old Yankee, I learned later, who was editor of the local Bugle. The man was just dropping off a package at the door stoop, but Margaret yelled out to him in her inelegant, stentorian voice: "Harvey, when are you going to become a Catholic?" I was taken aback a bit by this frontal approach. Margaret informed me years later that Harvey had eventually "taken instructions."

To make my suggestions for conversion tactics as brief as possible, I will just rattle off a list of approaches that are plain and undramatic but have proven considerably effective.

1. Pray for relatives and acquaintances to enter the Faith.

2. Know the Faith by reading solid spiritual books and periodicals.

3. Do not hesitate to let people in on the *supernatural* motives that govern your attitudes, decisions, and practices. (Don't tell people that daily Mass just "gives you something to do.")

4. Overcome inhibitions to "talk shop," that is, to discuss matters of your Church's morality and beliefs.

5. Ask close non-Catholic friends if they would like to borrow your Catholic literature.

6. Invite a close non-Catholic friend to an Easter or Christmas Mass, a funeral, a wedding.

7. Welcome a close non-Catholic friend to pray the Rosary with you in your home or to accompany you to public devotions.

8. Without being a litter-bug, try to leave Catholic pamphlets about in public places such as terminals and public conveyances.

9. Discriminately join in neighborhood non-sectarian Bible study or shared-prayer groups.

10. Steer clear of people who want merely to argue about religion, and at all times bear a humble mind toward those outside the Faith.

These suggestions, I realize, are hardly eye-openers; but

the fact is, they work. They work even in this age of communication overkill, "mod" priests and sisters, mad pursuit of the occult and bizarre in religion. They work because men still have a primitive and naive need for *le bon Dieu*, the good God. But it is likewise a simple, perennial truth that *le Dieu a besoin des hommes*, God needs men. To spread abroad and share with the world the "Beauty ever ancient, ever new," God, in his merciful Providence, needs middlemen—needs sheepdogs of the Good Shepherd and hounds of Heaven.

Argument from Causality

You two hundred men, who have come aside awhile
    To rest, you plumbers and dentists, you rank and file,
    Forsaking nets, you have come to barter bunks
    For beds and live three wordless days like monks:
    One has seen the evidence of invisible graces
    In your caged but patient gait, your love-sick faces.

No stealthy revels, no smuggled drafts of wine
    Have looped your lips or shot your cheeks with shine;
    No novel gospel or frantic ranting has whipped
    Your souls to too great zeal: a priest, soft-lipped,
    But told again God's blessings and behests,
    While Christ in the Host consoled his three-day guests.

Your brave retreat, your Tabor-time has flown.
So wonder not, in weeks, that fervid faith has blown
Away. Oh! wonder what, despite time's mists,
You proved one idle weekend: God exists!

7. Amazing Communication

OUR SUBJECT FOR this month's conference is a real bag of worms. But worms are indispensable for cultivation—even of the seeds of faith. Yes, from every angle, prayer is paradoxical. As fragile and precarious as a calla lily, prayer is universally conceded to be the bedrock of the spiritual life. It is constantly recommended and generally avoided. What is delightful and attractive to begin with proves repulsive and excruciating to persevere in. And for the spiritual writer, prayer poses an unavoidable but almost elusive topic of analysis and exhortation. In any age it would be difficult but necessary to fathom prayer or advocate its practice. To do so nowadays is especially urgent and at the same time uniquely problematic. Before directly grappling with the subject, I would like to touch upon three peculiar attitudes that militate against understanding or appreciating prayer in the twentieth century: disenchantment, insensibility, and self-consciousness.

Glancing over my jottings, I confess that I could fill a whole book documenting today's disenchantment. Our society is notoriously bankrupt in mystery, miracle, and majesty. Ellis (Albert) and Reubens have plucked Cupid's wings; Masters and Johnson have sterilized his arrow. Disneyland makes Fatima look bourgeois. Moonwalks have grown pedestrian. Jesus Christ now appears at best a befuddled radical, at worst the product of an LSD bummer. Lincoln seems to have been some admen's mosaic, not another Moses. Hollywood technicians can reproduce and divide a Red Sea, given a good location and a limitless budget. Little girls thwack electronic dolls. Little boys manhandle exquisite walkie-talkies. Drive-ins provide a production-line smorgasbord of exotic viands. Religious services here and there have taken on the look of fun and games. Elaborate happenings are mounted for the titillation of the well-to-do. Sports events and Broadway musicals are systematically manufactured, packaged, and sold like sausages for the less well-to-do. The old men's dreams are probably dirty dreams, and the young men's visions could easily be video-taped. Every person has a price; every product has a price-tag. We have grown mellow toward marvels; we wolf down wonders. The yawn and belch have replaced the gasp and sigh. This ennui, I contend, is not without its baneful effects on our understanding and evaluation of prayer. For prayer is a mysterious, miraculous form of communication with a Person of unspeakable majesty. If the telephone presents no cause for astonishment and admiration, putting in a direct call to God, which is what prayer essentially is, cannot be adequately estimated or properly esteemed. In due time, then, I will try to highlight the wonderful nature of prayer so as to countervail the disenchantment of the day.

Oddly enough, contemporaneous with this ho-hum attitude is a ceaseless hub-bub that drives us to distraction . . . and, ultimately, to insensibility. Subjected long enough to communication overkill in the shape, say, of aid-appeals, confrontation-politics, and assault-advertising, our ears begin to snap, crackle, and pop; and subliminally conditioned, we scream, "Will somebody turn off the bubble machine!" We grow sick of hearing about sickle-cells. Sibilant slogans in behalf of muscular dystrophy and systic fibrosis victims hiss through our dreams. Multi-colored hands of Biafrans and Bengalis, of Florentines and Peruvians, outstretch and engulf us like an octopus. Save a child. Hire the handicapped. Give a damn. Girl Scout Cookies. Peter's Pence. Fair Share. Have a heart. From our own hearts we eventually cry out, "Get off my back!" Then there are the spotlight-grabbers who in uninterrupted procession interrupt our lives: the yapping Yippies, the growling Panthers, the bellowing Birchites, the ad-libbing Women's Libbers, the palavering Playboys—and the whole boisterous lot of Neo-Nazi, Flower Children, Jesus Freaks, Serra Club, PYE, SNIC, SNAC, MOBE, GROPE, FLAB, FERN . . . kerplop!

But the grossest drubbing inflicted upon our sensibility has to come from the advertisement industry. They have turned our brains to jelly with an endless spate of nonsense words, like fixitives, additives, calmatives, whiteners, brighteners, free optionals, and beef by-products. They have reduced us to quivering hypochondriacs cautioning us about halitosis, houseitosis, pyorrhea, diarrhea, seborrhea, staph infection, and dental plaque. They have made soft drinks like Coke and Pepsi sound as important as sanctifying grace and pain-killers like Bayer's and Anacin as consoling as a good conscience. The upshot of all such communication overkill is that we are subtly conditioned to turn off exterior reality for sheer psychological survival. And this schizophrenic response to communication, I am sure, spills over into the communication called prayer. Our mental antennas become bent and corroded; we are rendered poor listeners for the Holy Spirit and impatient petitioners of the Divine Bounty. The very vocabulary, oral or mental, of our prayers is insidiously sapped of meaning and honesty. When words are a glut on the market, inflation sets in even in the realm of supernatural commerce. Hence I intend to spell out the prerequisite conditions and the details of the process whereby we pray, for these involve tuning out and turning up.

The third prevailing attitude that vitiates our appreciation of prayer is self-consciousness, that is, contemporary man's preoccupation with man and the things of man. Naturally, we are all men and, in the words of Plautus, nothing human should be alien to us. But today even religion is shot through with anthropocentricity. The so-called horizontal approach to the Divine has all but ousted the traditional vertical access to God. As an oft-quoted adage of the day has it: "I sought my soul; my soul I could not see. I sought my God; my God eluded me. I sought my neighbor, and I found all three." So far, so good: the times are out of joint, and perhaps the ABC's of communication must be consciously mastered before we can communicate with God. But my question is, Where do we go from there, after we have "found all three"? Do we still squander time and energy that should be spent sequestering ourselves with God on T-groups, sensitivity sessions, and parapsychology communes? Do we go on substituting group discussion for meditation? Not on bread or brotherhood alone does man live. Rollo May is not an adequate substitute for Saint Paul. The *I Ching* is not the inspired Word of God. And losing yourself, not finding yourself, is the ultimate goal of Christian asceticism. Many horizontal Christians would virtually have us reverse the order of the two Great Commandments. As long as self-knowledge and inter-personal experiments hold top priority in one's life, prayer will remain an irrelevant oddity of ambiguous value. Therefore I will have to stress, in the third part of the body of this conference, the unique importance of the transcendent communication that is prayer.

To recapitulate and project, I maintain that three present-day conditions prejudice our understanding and appreciation of prayer: namely, disenchantment, insensitivity, and self-consciousness. Furthermore, I believe that a careful consideration of the what, the how, and the why of prayer can dissipate these prejudices and contribute to our grasp and esteem of prayer. In my concluding paragraphs, I hope to delineate the milestones and obstacles in the life of prayer—to outline not only the introduction to, but the plot and denouement of, the devout life.

To explain the wonderful nature of prayer, I would first illustrate and analyze communication in general and then spiritual communication in particular. Almost every form of communication is mysterious and miraculous when you stop to think about it. The point is, you must wonder about it a while to see how wonderful it is. Some years ago I witnessed a television show on which Dunninger, perhaps the most famous mind-reader of recent memory, from a studio in New York had Senator Taft, a man of probity if ever there was one, withdraw a book from an enormous bookshelf, turn to a random page, and mentally scan any paragraph. Dunninger immediately recited, almost verbatim, the passage Taft had chosen. The Senator stood in a studio located in Washington, D.C.! But is it any the less marvelous that the thoughts and words the Senator meditated had been mentally telegraphed *to him* across the Atlantic Ocean and four centuries from the mind of Sir Francis Bacon through the medium of the printed page? Even in 1972 it would, doubtless, evoke more than a whistle of admiration to behold a forty-year-old corpse sit up and start crooning "*O sole mio.*" But is it much less awesome to resurrect just (!) the voice of Enrico Caruso by means of the phonograph? In the environs of every large city a Babel of disembodied voices divulge all the major events of the world not rarely, as in a seance, but every hour on the hour. To divine these radio newscasts sometimes requires no more paraphernalia than a filled tooth.

Essentially, the process of communication consists of three elements: a sender, a medium, and a receiver. (There are other factors, obviously: for example, the message, that which is communicated, whether a verbalized fact, coded prognostication, gestured command, or indicated emotion.) The functions of the sender and receiver are self-evident; the medium renders the former *present* to the latter.

If you can perceive that the natural communication which brings *General Hospital* into a million particular parlors is astonishing, then you may be prepared to grant that any instance of supernatural communication is stupifying. Prayer struck me as being a stark prodigy one humdrum day when I was in my first year of Theology. The time was a wee, small hour in a lazy spring afternoon; the place, a dismal church attached to our monastery - parish - kindergarten complex in the dreary town of Butler, New Jersey. Some odd errand had brought me to the sacristy, whence I overheard the inconceivable communication. There in the unlit church knelt forty assorted kindergarten children piping the Our Father with one unfaltering voice, and I knew by faith that the Lord God of Hosts was captive in the playpen of the sanctuary. I saw in a flash that every pious ejaculation was a celestial postcard, every meditation was an audience with the Almighty, every holy ambition was a coded cable to the Creator, every Rosary was a hot-line to Heaven.

Under analysis prayer proves to be one kind of communication that uses no medium, whether the message be the gesture of a good deed, the murmur of a formula, a cry of the heart, or a resolution of the mind. For God is ubiquitous; and if he is present to all of us at all times, then we are similarly present to him: "Woman, believe me, the hour is coming when neither on this mountain nor in Jerusalem will you worship the Father . . . God is spirit and they who worship him must worship in spirit and in truth" (Jn. 4:21, 24). To send God a message, we need only advert to him, only switch on our awareness of his proximity. So let us move on to consider the sender and receiver in supernatural communication.

The sender, of course, is a human being—or, as the yokel has it, a human bean. In the grand scheme of things the yokel's designation seems the more accurate description. For any conglomerate of individuals doesn't amount to a hill of beans. Man is but a flyspeck on a city map, an atom in the cosmos. The most important of the species are just a few syllables in history's *Who's Who*, some milliseconds on a carbon-clock. Man is a fluctuating five-dollars' worth of chemicals, a sixteenth-note on a flute in a symphony concert, a little stir in the mud. And so the Psalmist asked, "What is man that thou art mindful of him, the son of man that thou visitest him?" Still, he is made to the image and likeness of the Creator. The hairs on his head are divinely calculated; the contents within it constitute an inimitable galaxy of memories. His finger- and voice-prints are nonpareil. He is somebody's baby. And so Hamlet exclaimed, "What a piece of work is man! how noble in reason! how infinite in faculties!"

In prayer this "paragon of animals" makes contact with the Pure Spirit that puffed him to life. Unfortunately, the anthropomorphisms of the Iron Age and the electronic images of the Cybernetic Era have conditioned us to envision the receiver of our prayer as some fuss-budgety old man or a chrome-covered computer purring away out there. Hence the ooh and the ah have disappeared from our devotions. But a careful rereading of the yellowed Testaments can galvanize our conception of the Divine Majesty. The voice in the whirlwind confided to Job that the Leviathan was God's rubber ducky. In a vision Isaiah winced before a terrible Wizard of Oz. For the Psalmist the globe was God's footstool. It is no small thing, then, to pray and thus bend the ear of God to earth. A few weeks ago I read an interview in the *New York Times Sunday Supplement* granted by exiled Ezra Pound. One would think that the writer had been given an audience by Shakespeare reincarnated, so agog was he over and after the interview. Is it any less awe-inspiring to visit God in his study by the prayer of faith? Pound himself conceded that his communications were so much baby's babble; but even God's throat-clearing carries the sound of many waters.

Both within and outside the hour of prayer, the wonderful receiver of our communication may turn sender. We communicate with God by prayer; he communicates with us by inspiration, that is, by actual graces. Never have I met a person who would deny that he has experienced interiorly some uncanny lucid interval or been surprised by some sudden surge of resolution to behave better. As torrents in summer, half dried in their courses, suddenly rise, so the illumination of old spiritual truths and the energizing of latent good intentions strike us, as it were, from out of the blue. This is God, the Holy Spirit, reciprocating our prayer.

If prayer may be regarded as a sort of direct line to God ("Hello, Central, give me Heaven."), then I believe the telephone regulations that occasionally preface the Directory can shed some light on the prerequisites of prayer. If memory serves me, one set of rules for telephone etiquette went like this. "The caller will please speak to the other party promptly and listen attentively for the duration of the call. He will please address the other party in moderate tones and polite terms. He will take the other party seriously and not regard the communication as a joke. He will put through calls only as often and as long as they are necessary." These are not bad directives for dialing the Divinity.

When we talk vocally or mentally to God we should be sincere, not disguising our voice and making out we are Winston Churchill nor pretending it is an emergency when we are just killing time. If we are half-hearted in devotion and doubtful in our declaration, at least we can be decisive and forthright in confessing this fact to God. The other Party expects neither formalized posturing nor self-induced feverishness. Don't play the phoney when you telephone God. Fear ye not, and let it all hang out.

To quote an old pun, you can't tell-a-phone from a street-car. To be attentive in prayer, we must go "aside and rest awhile." If we find difficulty conversing with God, nine times out of ten it is due to the strident voices, street noises, and kaleidoscopic chaos surrounding us. Just as it is

Amazing Communication 73

easier to get a clear connection on a long-distance line in the cool, cool, cool of the evening, so we can make contact with God in prayer only after we have withdrawn from the maddening crowd, forgotten worldly concerns, and calmed our harried souls. Even to entertain the conviction of God's existence necessitates creeping into our heart of hearts: "Be still, and know that I am God." It was simplistic of me, I know, to heed the Gospel summons literally when I was a teenager and to actually crouch in my clothes closet to pray; but I am inclined to believe that my communication with God at that point in my life was a lot less distracted than ever after.

If a telephone call calls for certain civilities, prayer no less demands a proper politeness. And the only polite stance for us human beans is one of humility. God, we are told, resists the proud and gives grace to the humble. Hardly ever did Jesus fail to reward an admission of unworthiness with a word of praise, an instant miracle, or a spiritual boon. Thus he made an apostle of Peter upon a confession of sinfulness; he cured from afar the daughter of the Canaanite woman who reckoned herself a dog; and he lauded the paradigm Publican at the back of the Temple. But our prayer must also be bold and confident, even as we are generally not deceived in trusting that the other party on our local line is there and listening sympathetically. The clever quip echoed by many a preacher contradicts the Gospel: "God answers every prayer; sometimes the answer is No." Jesus' version has no such quibble: "Whatsoever you ask in prayer, believing, you shall receive." God will not yawn or cover the ear-piece. So ring him up anytime and order anything: ask, knock, seek; and it will be given pressed down and overflowing. The only string attached is that we must be prepared to live with what we have procured in prayer.

The final condition for spiritual communication is frequency. The typical paterfamilias, if he can afford it, is forced to provide his little princess with a princess telephone because she practically has the family line in shreds. College dormers, despite the generation gap, do more than their share to raise the value of AT&T stock by calling home every week. So, if God is our Father and we were made to know, love, and serve him, the proverb, *"Out of sight is out of mind,"* should not obtain in our prayer life. Rather, it should be a case of absence making the heart grow fonder; and we should ring him up at least once a day. Sometimes a real gab session is in order. Remember, even in prayer the overtime rates go down; and at any rate, God picks up the charges. The Bell System must take a back seat to the celestial system, too, inasmuch as your call will never keep another party waiting nor ever be impeded because "the lion is busy."

As to the question of why we must pray, there is a simple and a subtle answer. Let us begin with the more obvious motives. In all honesty it would seem that a person need not communicate with God if . . . If he has never fallen short of the will of God, if he has never sinned. But if he has faltered and does falter, he must pray: for love means having to say "I'm sorry" (Sorry about that, Eric Segal). If he stands in need of nothing, he can avoid God. But if he has crying needs and unfulfilled dreams, if he is "blessed" like Daniel the "man of desires" (Dn. 10:11), he must pray: for to take one giant step forward very often God stipulates that we say, "May I?" If he is conscious of no gratuitous endowments like good health or literacy, he can hold his peace. Otherwise, he must pray: for no further gum-drops will be dropped into his lap without his simple "Thank you." If he is blind to God's grandeur in the seasons or unimpressed with his innocence as revealed in his saints, he may be spiritually mum. Otherwise, he must pray: for prayer or worship (A.S. "worth-ship") is but the heart instinctively crying out "Holy Mackerel!"

Of course, the most compelling reason for praying is a

Amazing Communication

subtle one. It defies articulation not because it is vague and flimsy like a cobweb, but because it is many-faceted and impenetrable like a diamond. Not even Shakespeare could pinpoint the attraction of prayer, for some moments of spiritual communication offer a foretaste of what eye has not seen or ear heard. For those who have never experienced this visitation, no explanation is possible; for those who have experienced it, no explanation is necessary: "Taste and see that the Lord is sweet" (Ps. 33:9). But the most worldly of us, before we have advanced far in life, can come to the realization that "the eye is not filled with seeing and the ear is not filled with hearing" (Eccl. 1:8). It is but a short step from there to learn that "our hearts, O Lord, were made for thee." We were made to see God face to face in Heaven. Is it surprising that the soul should thrill to glimpse his face here below as through a lattice in a moment of meditation? Much of the activity and endeavor connected with church and religion is necessary work, but it is mere busy-work in comparison to searching for God in prayer; finding him, and this alone, validates all the rest of our hustling homage. Without renewed communication with the Lord, we will soon find ourselves only going through the motions of devotions. But the temptation to observe every religious obligation except prayer can grow irresistibly strong. This eventuality usually arises when we have been spiritually weaned in meditation and induced to seek the God of consolations instead of the consolations of God. And so the discussion of the ultimate motive for prayer takes us to the final consideration of this conference—the spiritual odyssey that is the life of prayer.

Actually, we have been considering prayer as an act It is quite another and far more difficult thing to explain the life of prayer; for it is almost as complex, variegated, and personalized as a life itself. What I shall say here is based partly on many spirituality books I have read since my novitiate and partly upon personal experience with prayer. It is impossible for me to trace more precisely than this the sources of my observations on the life of prayer.

Usually one begins the devout life by getting absorbed in and drawing unction from vocal prayers and church services. He starts to prolong his private "devotions" and likes to "drop into" a church at an odd moment as well as to arrange "quiet times" for himself in the privacy of his room. Next, with the help of spiritual literature or a sensitive confessor, he proposes and pursues some form of regular meditation period. After an initial term of difficulty—the trouble implicit in overcoming the inertia hindering the formation of any good habit—meditation becomes consistently profitable and satisfying, though not always gratifying. Then anywhere between six months and two years after one has become proficient in meditation, something snaps. Quite abruptly God seems to "pull a Houdini" on the suppliant who means business. He not only seems to disappear, but he also sees to it that the moments of discursive prayer become unaccountably and unnaturally painful. At this juncture, if a person has sufficient pretext—in the form of a welter of other obvious obligations, such as study or service—he will leave off meditating with great relief. If he is of an heroic bent and unshakably convinced of the absolute value of mental prayer, he will apply himself to his spiritual reading and meditation hour with spartan determination. But both devout souls, the weakling and the hero, will probably find themselves drawn or impelled to make random, satisfying contact with the Almighty at various intervals for the next fifteen or twenty years. In the meantime they may resort to all sorts of devotions, long or short, frequently or by fits and starts, such as Rosaries, Stations, ejaculations, uplifting literature, shared-prayers, Bible vigils, five-minute reflections, chapel visits, or conference-writing—all this in an attempt to substitute for mental prayer, now a long-lost art. During the next

Amazing Communication

and last phase of the devout life (after twenty years, it is said), even all forms of spiritual busy-work grow distasteful; and the one-time friend of God seriously considers himself an outcast from the Lord. Jesus seems like a dim wraith from the past; his first sweet summons to the devout life all but rings like a heckle through the corridors of memory. Let it be said, however, that all through this prayer-lifetime and apart from exceptional lapses that may occur here and there, the person is careful to avoid deliberately offending God, is seriously devoted to the duties of his state in life, frequents the sacraments, and has a vague but all-pervasive dissatisfaction with creatures (not excluding his confreres and community, if his is a professed religious). Many prayer adepts are at this juncture called to meet their Maker—and this without much delay, since they have spent their Purgatory on earth. A few are visited with exceptional lights and consolations in rare moments of infused contemplation, which is an indescribable direct experiencing of God. But both the ordinary and the extraordinary perseverer in prayer may be characterized in this final phase of their prayer-life as suffering an enduring heartache for God.

Actually, and wonderful to tell, the several roadblocks in the course of prayer—whatever their precise label, aridity, or night of the senses, desolation or night of the spirit—constitute milestones and are to be secretly relished, not lamented. To change the metaphor for a minute, if the prayer-life were likened to a canoe ride up the river, one might make strenuous efforts to paddle against the current and make no headway, the scenery on the banks remaining monotonously the same. But the mere fact that the environment does not alter argues to the fact that the praying oarsman is performing manfully. And God, at his own sweet time and in his own incalculable way, can wonderfully transform the scenery on the banks in the twinkling of an eye.

Obviously and admittedly, I cannot vouch for every item

in the itinerarium of the soul to God, but I do have a few simple convictions on the subject of prayer-life; and with them I shall conclude this rather long and serpentine sermon. I do believe that prayer is the whole ball of wax in the spiritual life and that often it proves as jejune and sticky and pliant as a ball of wax. Of prayer, I say what Hamlet said: "The readiness is all"; that is, one must be disposed to pray even if the disposition of things make conscious prayer seemingly and humanly speaking impossible. In the last analysis, to want to pray, to sincerely wish to pray, is prayer—perhaps the subtlest, sinewiest, most unsatisfying (but most satisfactory) kind of prayer. Underlying our every spasmodic and sporadic effort to contact God, the essential virtue of Hope is operative, and the Holy Spirit "pleads within us with unutterable groanings" (Rom. 8:26). The one roadblock that does indeed block the journey of the soul to God through prayer is despair. To put it another way, prayer is not the lifting up of the mind and heart to God, as the old catechism would have it; prayer is the lifting up of the mind and/or heart to God. The only obstacle to this rarified *sursum corda* is genuine discouragement. So, in whatever way, at whatever times, with whatever apparent effect, let us not cease to attempt to maintain contact with God in spiritual communication.

The most miraculous feature of prayer, finally, is that, to this day, it is the only form of communication that is simultaneously a form of transportation: the direct line to God is also an elevator cable. Or so Saint Paul would lead us to believe: "Mind the things that are above, not the things that are on earth. For you have died and your life is hidden with Christ in God. When Christ, your life, shall appear, then you will appear *with him* in glory" (Col. 3:3-4).

A Wise Goose Chase

*There was a time when music moved my soul
With melodies divine, but I was wrong:
Some lovely Dove and mellow did cajole,
Was cooing, wooing me to some purer song.
Once all wild fields and wakeful forests stirred
My heart with a swishing spirit, made it quest
For what I knew not (know now for a Bird
Who nurtures life, yet nestles all to rest).
Designs of science then my mind could thrill;
My banks of books held wisdom's wealth untold.
Still, in that breathless height I saw Him still—
What form! What feathers! argent but for gold.*

*Come, Dove, Who leafed then left what I loved most,
Perch on my barren branches, O Holy Ghost!*

8. *The Charms of Chastity*

THE TOPIC OF this month's conference is the vow and virtue of chastity. For several years now I've been hankering to give "a local habitation and a name" to my position on this currently unpopular commitment. Recent best-sellers and rock musicals have brazenly propounded an amatory Christ. We are still witnessing a minor exodus from the priesthood and the religious life. A deluge of publications directed to the Sensuous Man, Woman, and Child threatens. But none of these has sufficiently piqued me into attempting this long overdue apology for the celibate life. No, it was a sentiment casually voiced last Christmas, when over the vacation I attended a reunion with some of my dearest high school chums. As we sipped coffee and nibbled Stella d'Oro cookies, my one-time girl friend—now a happily married mother of three and still devout daughter of the Church (and still a visual "knockout," I might add)—maintained it was self-evident that priests ought to marry. This was the last straw! In a flash there swam into my mind fond images of Dr. Gifford, the cultured pastor; Fr. Cornell, the troubleshooter; Fr. Daniels, the jolly old soul; and Fr. Wren, the priests' priest—each of whom had sweetly and indelibly nurtured the faith of four of us at that table, thanks largely to their lives of vowed celibacy. I resolved then and there sometime soon to "tell it like it is" about chastity once and for all.

And I confess that it takes considerable resolve to write sympathetically about chastity, for it is a delicate and elusive

The Charms of Chastity

subject that few have adequately explained. The reason for the customary reticence or inevitable vagueness on the matter is twofold. On the one hand, the classical (and facile) definition of the vow of chastity is couched in negative terms exclusively, whereas the virtue is every bit as positive as charity, which is hardly summed up as a series of "Thou shalt not's." On the other hand, the positive value of chastity—though very real, rich, and rational—is as subjective, subtle, and sublime as one's reasons for choosing a particular life-partner in marriage, which motives are not exactly exhausted by the formula, "He (she) doesn't drink, smoke, or run around." In short, it is almost as impossible and as embarrassing for me to put down in cold print what this vow means to me as it would be for a husband to publicly articulate all of his wife's unique charms. But I feel that the life of consecrated celibacy is under fire; and, if only for the enlightenment of my old flame, I'm impelled to present the case for chastity as best I can. This product of my lucubrations will fall into three sections: an exposition of what the vow entails and a review of how Jesus practiced and counselled chastity as well as a rationale of why chastity may not, like love, make the world go round but does help it spiral upwards.

Good exposition moves from the more familiar to the less familiar. Unfortunately for the apologist, what is most obvious about the vow of chastity is also what is most objectionable, most negative. The vow explicitly enjoins abstention in two precise areas and implicitly prescribes caution in two wider realms. When a person professes the vow of chastity, he makes a solemn and life-long promise to God not to marry and not to indulge in any sexual pleasure. To the end of keeping this promise, he likewise obliges himself to avoid dangerous and exclusive involvements with persons of the opposite sex as well as to maintain control over all his sensual appetites. Admittedly, this regimen, especially as expressed in such legal and latinate generalities (the last, I hope, of this conference) sounds positively gruesome. Upon closer inspection and fleshed out with illustration, it proves not so awfully inhuman. So let us examine one by one these four provisions of the vow of chastity.

Occasionally I have eavesdropped on lobbyists for a connubial clergy, and now and then played captive audience to some lovely young thing lecturing on the evils of bachelorhood. All have given me the distinct impression that (1) the priest or religious belongs to a peculiar and medieval minority and (2) the rest of the human race is advancing by leaps and bounds in wisdom, age, and grace as an unfailing consequence of matrimonial beatitude. But a little reflection will show that the unusual minority is neither very exotic nor exactly minute. Many unmonkish professionals such as Beethoven and Alec Guinness have opted for celibacy; many uncloistered career women from Jane Austen to Willa Cather have preferred to remain unattached for life. Thousands of unprofessed brothers and sisters with all their emotional "marbles" and with their eyes wide open have foregone marriage to care for incapacitated parents. Millions of "parents without partners" are bravely making a go of it living in virtual celibacy. And perhaps a billion souls are leading normal, healthy lives minus the marital counterpart they have either lost or not yet found. Finally, granting that the Good Book is more reliable than Bobby Burns's love lyrics, it must be conceded that the citizens of the New Jerusalem very likely are not given to celebrating wedding anniversaries (Lk. 20:35). Look at the other side of the coin. A glance at the vital statistics or a smattering of marriage-counselling experience will show that the rest of the race hardly presents an object lesson in self-fulfillment. In the United States three out of ten marriages end in divorce; and another three reach a stage, it would seem, that can literally be termed a stalemate. Regrettably, the institution is presently under such constant assault from all quarters that it ill behooves a complacent cleric to add his two cents' worth. I will simply say that, prescinding from a vocation to the state and the grace of the sacrament, Francis Bacon's witticism rings ten times truer in the reign of Elizabeth II: "He who hath a wife and children hath delivered hostages to Fortune." I little expect that these unromantic animadversions will send legions scurrying to the convent, thanks to the perennial marksmanship of Dan Cupid. But I do hope they will deter a few faint hearts from inching toward the monastery exit, drawn by the siren song of "pop" theologians.

What C. J. Martindale calls "The Difficult Commandment" ordinarily comes no easier to us mortals under vows. It is also difficult, I find, to write appreciatively about the second stipulation of the vow of chastity—abstention from all sexual pleasure. Sexuality is a mysterious and many-faceted subject, one which I barely fathom and certainly cannot adequately explore here. Yet I would like to address a few remarks to those who tend to exaggerate, minimize, or scruple over this biological iceberg (hot ice, if you will).

Admittedly, there was a time when chicken breasts and legs had to be re-christened light meat and dark meat, and when God-fearing physicians were routinely invoked to attest to the ravages attendant upon sexual experimentation. But it is equally undeniable that this period of militant prudery was closed with a vengeance and followed by three decades wherein pan-sexuality ruled the counsellor's roost, psychoanalysis became a national parlor game, and psychiatry and religion plainly grew polarized. Even today, unmitigated Freudianism lingers on among noted psychiatrists such as Albert Ellis and paperback profiteers like Dr. Reubens (despite the substantial amendments of Jung, Adler, and Reik as well as the successful non-libidinal approaches taken to psychological problems by Rogers, Bettleheim, and

Lorenz). The vowed religious must still be circumspect in seeking psychiatric help, lest he be assured that sexual abstinence, unquestionably, is harmful if not immoral or impossible. These neo-Freudians are deceived not only in locating all of man's hangups somewhere below the belt but also in pinning his affections to the erogenous zones.

Do not mistake my drift. I am not challenging the elemental importance of sex: fifty million Frenchmen—and three billion Earthmen—can't be wrong. But I do insist that there isn't a shred of evidence that the prolonged practice of abstinence (on the part of an emotionally sound religious) has ever proven fatal, that priests are not jettisoning their vows (if we may believe Andrew Greeley) because of the impossibility of continence, and that sexual appetite (despite its obvious urgency) is a "sometime thing," as sporadic and finite as the need to fill one's stomach. Chastity is not the root of all evil.

To judge from certain ascetical manuals and occasional rec-room post-mortems, there are also some lingering myths that grossly belittle the enormous sacrifice implicit in practicing sexual abstention. Some spiritual counsellors still would have it that the less fussing over this particular vow, the better; that with the taking of the vow temptations will abate; and that "the pilot light" will unquestionably go out if one perseveres till middle-age. These offer as a solution at once to cold feet and ardent urges simply a cold shower; and they caution in vague, minor tones about the insidious man-trap of "particular friendships." In the light of this simplistic view, not-so-charitable survivors of the exodus opine that so-and-so left because he had "hot pants" or never could "keep his hands to himself" or always "wore his heart on his sleeve." All such modern-day Pelagians must be re-apprised of the radical holocaust chastity entails and made to own up to the need of completely revolutionizing religious and clerical life-styles to render that sacrifice physically possible as well

The Charms of Chastity

as psychologically profitable. As in all worthwhile revolutions, the revitalization will be a revival: a revival of the genuine camaraderie of the Apostles and pioneer religious groups, a revival of low-stress routine (special priority being given to spiritual recuperation), a revival of conscientious recreation in common, and a revival of down-to-earth, homegrown, unfeigned openness between subjects and superiors and among one's peers. All the help that reputable psychology and psychiatry can proffer, too, should be sought and sampled without hesitation. It takes a heap of living to keep a convent or rectory from becoming a neurotics' ward.

Then there are those for whom the vow of chastity may become temporarily or periodically a needless but serious cause for alarm. Some of these harried souls are still nursing or have lately resurrected adolescent scrupulosity in regard to mental sins of impurity. If preoccupation with sexual fantasies borders on the compulsive or the guilt over entertaining them is out of all proportion with real culpability, the case is one for the psychiatrist. Otherwise, a little clarification should go a long way towards restoring a correctly informed conscience, and a measure of peace, to the scruple-ridden. First, the Devil is not lightly to be adduced as the inspirer of one's lascivious mental movies. Second, having "bad thoughts" is neither tantamount to entertaining them nor indicative of a condition any more serious than that of being "alive and kicking." And third, if one has not by word or act beforehand prompted or afterwards fulfilled these fantasies, he is very likely free of serious guilt. Finally, our Lord's warning about "lusting after a woman" in one's heart and thereby committing virtual adultery is to be construed as implying as strong and clear an evil intention as that of the bankrobber (of the paradigm) who is baffled in his execution only by the sudden appearance of unforeseen guards on the premises. As for those other beleaguered individuals who occasionally or for a longer stretch habitually give in to temptation and commit a sin of impurity, particularly a solitary sin, they should not be utterly shaken nor readily reach for their walking papers. On the one hand, the profession of vows does not render the sacrament of Penance for all practical purposes irrelevant or make the Holy Sacrifice of the Mass, dominated as it is with sin and redemption themes, personally pointless. And just as divorce is not the only logical alternative to the flawless marriage, so too partial infidelity to the vow of chastity hardly renders a vocation null and void or necessarily spells a decree of dispensation. On the other hand, constant bouts with temptations to impurity may very likely be regarded as symptomatic. They may telegraph to a priest or religious that something radical is amiss about his present apostolate or regimen of life; for such temptations arise almost inevitably from the fatigue and frustration that follow stressful irregularity and uncongenial employment, not to mention dangerous intimacy with the opposite sex. Before a monk begins monkeying with his vows, he had better calmly and coolly reason out his scruples and safely and sanely recapture his integrity.

Regarding the two implicit obligations stemming from the vow of chastity, I may be permitted to be short and sweet. For their import, though broad, is clear; and their importance, though clear, is indirect. From personal experience, I readily concede that living in an all-male community for any length of time has its psychic liabilities, and I suppose the same is true for a sister sequestered in her one-sex milieu. Men without women tend to grow shaggy of appearance and gruff of manner—ursine, in short. Women without men, I submit, are prone to formalism, indecision, and intrigue. But it is important to realize that these are liabilities: they are not fatalities in either of the two senses of the word. That is, these handicaps are not fated necessarily to materialize; and even if they do, they should not prove fatal to one's psyche.

Nowadays most people in vows, by dint of their active apostolate or at least through liberal contact with family, in all likelihood have more than sufficient dealings with the opposite sex to prevent psychological starvation, emotional imbalance, or gender-confusion. Then again, there is no lack of opportunity for intellectual and vicarious commerce with the opposite sex, thanks to the availability of literature and the mass media.

Some avant garde commentators on the religious scene, after exaggerating the aforementioned liabilities, have zealously propounded a solution they term the Third Way. This Third Way, according to them, lies somewhere between the path the married tread and the road those vowed to celibacy have traditionally traversed: to experience all the agonies and the ecstasies of deep, meaningful relationships with one (or a few) of the opposite sex to every extent short of romance and love-making. In my opinion, this middle path leads abruptly to a will-o'-the-wisp. For one thing, it seems to me that such demanding and fulfilling existential relationships, not mere biological satisfactions, are quintessentially what one sacrifices by taking the vow of celibacy. For another, I am personally convinced—having savored the joys and the jealousies of falling in love in my pre-seminary days—that sharing soul-secrets and sighs with one's opposite number can be as mind-blowing and as lethal as a dose of uncut heroin. I, for one, would eternally hesitate to be the guinea pig that had to prove the feasibility of the Third Way. I used to claim that if Elsa Maxwell and Pope John were locked up in the same cabin for two weeks, they would end up pitching woo. Since then the case history of every defecting priest I have known has only strengthened my conviction on the matter

Coming to the fourth and final stipulation of the vow, I have only this to remark in a general way about practicing mortification: what the world invariably applauds in the secular realm raises its darkest suspicions in the religious sphere. Call the phenomenon a paradox, if you will; I deem it a downright contradiction. What I mean is, people instinctively whistle in admiration at the sight of a gorgeous feminine physique such as that of Raquel Welch, the product, to a great extent, of spartan calisthenics by the seashore, but murmur in indignation upon learning of the rigorous schedule of the Poor Clares, whose pulchritude evokes the admiration of heavenly hosts. Moderns rankle to hear that fasting and the discipline cord have in some monasteries survived the thumb-screw and rack of the Middle Ages, but cheer to the echo the hard-won prowess of a Hank Aaron or the calloused stamina of a Johnny Unitas. Myopic mortals despise as lickspittle and unmanly the self-effacement and blind obedience of Trappist monks, but glow with pride over the discipline and teamwork of their Olympics representatives. In short everyone approves and admires mortification of the hand, heart, and head; but only a few are willing to endorse and commend such self-control when undertaken for supernatural motives. This double-standard outlook regarding abnegation probably arises from the fact that deep down in their hearts many nominal believers do not believe that this world and its glory are passing away, nor that eye has not seen and ear has not heard what good things God has prepared for those who love him with all their mind and heart and soul. They do not realize at gut-level, at any rate, that this earth is a training ground and that those vowed to self-denial in all its forms are merely cramming for their finals. Having ears, they do not hear that some have made themselves eunuchs for the sake of the Kingdom of Heaven.

These, then, are my musings about what the vow of celibacy entails. My subject matter has dictated the negative approach, since the four provisos are prohibitions—forbidding legitimate marriage, sexual indulgence, exclusive attachment, and self-gratification. In the next conference I propose to explore Jesus Christ's attitude toward chastity and the

The Charms of Chastity

positive dimensions of that virtue. For now I will close with a passage from the explanatory introduction from John Blofield's very popular paperback edition of the *I Ching*—the three-thousand-year-old "Book of Changes," which is hardly derivative from the Rule of Saint Benedict or *The Imitation of Christ*: "To the latter [a native of the Far East] extramarital sexual relations are culpable only if they cause suffering either to one of the persons concerned or to others: chastity becomes a moral duty only when a man undertakes to devote his entire energies to achieving the supreme goal— Enlightenment, Absorption in the Tao or whatever he may have learnt to call it" (p. 37).

The *vow* of chastity is a subject involving notions that are largely legal and negative—ideas that are quite objective, limited, and more or less traditional. The virtue of chastity, which the vow assumes, protects, and fosters, is a more poetic and positive matter—one so rich and subtle that it allows of only partial and personal treatment. Now, a person doesn't have to be a marksman to take a shot in the dark. So however ineffable the subject or inadequate the writer, I would like to try to analyze the charms of the virtue of chastity. First, I propose to examine the life of Jesus to show how he practiced and preached chastity in its highest degree; and then I would like to probe the essence of the virtue that underlies and rises from the vow.

According to immemorial traditions in the Church—traditions that the New Testament implicitly supports and in no way impugns—Jesus was born of a perpetual virgin (Mary), reared by a life-long virgin (Joseph), and baptized by a professed virgin (John). Jesus entrusted his Virgin Mother (who had no other children to care for her) to an Apostle (John) who is reputed to have been a life-long virgin and who recorded a vision of the Lamb of God leading about a train of male virgins in heaven (Rv. 14). Furthermore, Jesus was slavishly imitated, in life and in death, by an Apostle who was a self-confessed virgin (1 Cor. 7). Throughout his public life Jesus moved freely among women and was readily approached by women of ill repute. Nevertheless, the Master's enemies, who accused the man of irreverence and intemperance, never so much as hinted a charge against Jesus of sexual immorality. The Galahad from Galilee could hardly have induced the self-righteous vigilantes to drop their stones if he were living in a glass house.

Nor can we, by an odd twist, fault Jesus for not preaching what he practiced. First, the Lord was adamant in his teaching about marital chastity. He astounded his disciples by transcending even the well known precept of Shemmai, the conservative moralist who allowed divorce only on the grounds of adultery, and by insisting upon the absolute indissolubility of marriage (Mt. 19:3-10; 1 Cor. 7:8-9). He forbade lascivious desires and rigorously cautioned custody of the senses (Mt. 5:27-30). Then again, Jesus championed the innocence of children when he sternly threatened their would-be seducers (Mt. 18:6); he flatly rebuked the Apostles for shooing away these prototypes of celestial citizenry (Mt. 19:14). And on a number of occasions Jesus spoke in defense of fallen women who had regained their innocence by heartfelt repentance. Finally, our Lord invited anyone who by special vocation was so inclined, to pursue the Kingdom of God by foregoing the support and satisfaction not only of his present family (Mk. 10:29-31), but also of his potential family (Mt. 19:12). Jesus had himself become "a eunuch for the sake of the Kingdom of Heaven" and was a living testimony to the eschatological doctrine he later enunciated: "For at the resurrection they will neither marry nor be given in marriage, but will be as angels of God in heaven" (Mt. 22:30).

The unprecedented chastity Jesus propounded by his words and works to "an unbelieving and adulterous generation" is inextricably bound up with three fundamental

The Charms of Chastity

features of his sacred mission in the world: his loving availability, his prayerful apart-ness, and his life-germinating death. The Son of Man had no place to lay his head . . . or his heart. His whole public life was merely a succession of visits, a series of guest appearances, a sequence of encounters: at Cana, Capharnaum, Sichem, Gerasa, Bethsaida, Jericho, Bethany, Jerusalem, and Emmaus. From sun-up till well into the night Jesus was available to the sick and the seeker; he was all things to all men. Without domestic roots and free from familial ties, Jesus could make his mission an endless itinerary. Transient though he was, he left in his wake a chain of spiritual bonds among those who, having heard and performed the will of the Father in Heaven, had become by supernatural adoption Christ's brother, sister, and mother.

In spite of the nearly killing pace of the apostolate, not once did the Master appear in public emotionally harried, mentally distraught, or even physically depleted. No doubt his uncanny stamina and aplomb were due in great measure to the intervals, long or brief, that Jesus regularly devoted to solitary prayer, wherein he recouped spiritual and even bodily strength by partaking of that incorporeal bread to which he occasionally alluded. But such composure amid the hurly-burly of his public life was patently abetted by the personal detachment inherent in his celibate status, as were his very opportunities for prayerful retreat. Like the sacraments Jesus instituted, his virginity both signalled and effected the sacred apart-ness, the unprofane otherness of the Anointed. Accordingly, he who was all things to all men, was simultaneously *in* the world and not *of* it.

Neither the advocates nor the opponents of virginity will deny that the renunciation of sexual fulfillment in marriage is at least a minor crucifixion—a morbid and masochistic one in the eyes of some, to be sure. Now, from the prophecy of Simeon onward, the shadow of the Cross loomed across our Lord's life. The aforementioned visits of Jesus were all only watering stops in his march toward Calvary. Before the Man of Sorrows actually foretold his Passion and Death, he had projected the Crucifixion every time he summoned men to conversion and disciplehood with the unusual idiom: "Take up your cross, and follow me." At times he expressed the formula for salvation paradoxically: "He who will lose his life for my sake shall find it." His most graphic, most cogent appeal to mortification—one that again anticipates his Crucifixion—is couched in a metaphor of vegetative reproduction: "Unless the grain of wheat falls into the ground and dies, it remains alone. But if it dies, it brings forth much fruit" (Jn. 12:24-25). Thus we can see in view of our Lord's understanding of renunciation, especially that existential denial involved in complete chastity, his life was filled with not only the foreknowledge but also the foretaste of his redeeming Death. Biologically sterile (for the sake of the Kingdom), Jesus became the mystical Seed that was planted in the earth for three days and sprang up as the living Vine on Easter morning. This Vine has mounted to heaven and will ultimately provide passage, to alter the figure a bit, for every man-jack of us who will ascend to the Father's mansions. In life-germinating death alone do we see the full significance of the virtue of chastity so prominent in the biography of Jesus.

Down through the centuries *anno domini*, thousands upon thousands have successfully imitated Jesus in his fruitful renunciation of marriage and sexual satisfaction: parish priests, contemplative nuns, tireless missionaries, teaching sisters, diligent monks, inconspicuous lay-brothers, telephone operators in lay institutes, nurses in private vows, and myriads of devout sons and daughters and parents-without partners who have resigned themselves to serving their parents and children in virtual virginity. Their lives have not been negative and unproductive. A power has gone out from them. Of each of them it can be claimed, as Tennyson said of Sir Galahad: "His strength is as the strength of ten because his heart is pure." And it remains for us to see what essentially constitutes this beneficent and positive virtue of chastity. To my mind, chastity is a composite virute, an organic blend of three interrelated qualities of soul: viz., compassion, innocence, and idealism. To my way of thinking, moreover, each of these three qualities has two distinct, shining facets.

To show the intimate connection between chastity and compassion, I would first like to collate two passages of Scripture. In delineating the Suffering Servant, Isaiah wrote: "If he shall lay down his life for sin, he shall see a long-lived seed, and the will of the Lord shall be prosperous in his hand. Because his soul has labored, he shall see and be filled. By his knowledge shall this my just servant justify many, and shall bear their iniquities" (Is. 53:10-11). The author of the Epistle to the Hebrews obviously had this description in mind when he remembered the Redeemer who had been both High Priest and Victim: "For we have not a High Priest who cannot have compassion on our infirmities, but one tried as we are in all things except sin. Let us therefore draw near with confidence to the throne of grace, that we may obtain mercy and find grace to help in time of need" (Heb. 4:15-16). As we have already seen, by virtue of his virginity, Jesus had a constant reminder and foretaste of his Passion. His habitual *com*passion—manifested to the point of open weeping on the occasion of the funeral of a widow's only son, the bereavement of Martha and Mary, and the preview of Jerusalem's destruction—not only issued in his Crucifixion but also sprang from the forepangs of that crucifixion involved in his practice of chastity. Only a fellow sufferer can genuinely sympathize with the suffering; all others are to a certain extent simply Job's counselors. The tenderheartedness of the chaste is almost proverbial. It explains why the doleful race of Irish hasten to take their problems to the local dominee, even if he be addicted to "the crayture." It explains why priest-chaplains can strike peace into a panicky foxhole. It explains why religious sisters are such a welcome sight at the graveside of "an athlete dying young." It explains why stipends for Gregorian Masses are regularly dispatched to Benedictine and Trappist monks. It explains, finally, why Catholics and many non-Catholics instinctively head for the nearest convent or rectory when smarting from "the slings and arrows of outrageous fortune and the thousand natural shocks that flesh is heir to."

If one studies this fire-tried compassion at work in each of the two sexes, he will discover that it assumes two distinct complexions. For want of a more accurate word, I would call male compassion tenderness tinged with chivalry, which the dictionary defines as "the qualities of a knight, such as courage, nobility, fairness, courtesy, respect of women, protection of the poor, etc." What Lacordaire so eloquently said of the priest's vocation (which applies, *mutatis mutandis*, to lay brothers) is redolent of the galant's code of life:

> To live in the midst of the world without wishing its pleasures; to be a member of each family, yet belonging to none; to share all sufferings; to penetrate all secrets; to heal all wounds; to go from men to God and offer Him their prayers; to return from God to men to bring pardon and hope; to have a heart of fire for charity and a heart of bronze for chastity; to teach and to pardon, console and bless always—what a glorious life!

Speaking for myself, and from over twelve years of experience in the priesthood, I can affirm that many people with problems, especially ladies in distress, regard men under vows as knights errant to whom they may have recourse anytime and anywhere in almost any emergency. My unofficial ministry has brought me into homes for unwed mothers, women's prisons, swanky apartments, flop-houses, store-front churches, and A. A. meeting places. My gallantry has cost me here and there a wristwatch, some collect-call expenses, many hours of chauffeuring, two transistor radios, bus fares, hotel expenses, many hours of counselling, and some sleep-robbed nights—the list is not exhaustive. Sometimes "What a glorious life" has an ironic ring for me and my fellow friars. Compassion in women religious, on the other hand, is mingled with what I can only call motherliness. Naturally, the apostolates of many sisters call for and in fact evoke maternal compassion: kindergartens, orphanages, old-age homes, hospitals, asylums for the mentally ill or retarded, clinics, leprosariums, parochial schools, colleges, catechism classes, and social work (all still vivid evidence, in her post-conciliar age, of one of the four marks of the Church—holiness). But over and above these obvious exercises in motherliness, there are many subtler and more informal instances of maternal concern on the part of women in vows, such as among Poor Clares and other contemplatives who day and night avert God's righteous indignation from his sinful children and among all the big-hearted "good sisters" to whom relatives and acquaintances, particularly the menfolk, turn for prayers and consolation in "impossible cases."

Innocence is the next component of chastity to be considered. Now, just as the virtue of chastity is something more than the absence of lust, so too is innocence, in my opinion, more substantial than a lack of guilt, as the first dictionary meaning would have it. We all loosely concede that when children metamorphose into adults, they generally lose something; and I contend that one cannot speak of losing a lack of something without considerable violence to the language and the mind. And so, assuming a rather self-evident relatedness between innocence and chastity, I prefer to explore first another dictionary meaning of the term and then to elaborate an original but reasonable explanation of the nature of innocence.

If ever movies were eternally worthy of a GP rating, surely such are *Snow White and the Seven Dwarfs*, *Pinocchio*, and *The Wizard of Oz*. Whenever these masterpieces are re-released, flocks of families press to the box offices as if on a pilgrimage. Parents are in hopes, I suspect, not only of reliving with their children an experience of innocent enjoyment but also of inculcating in them and recapturing for themselves the distinct joy of innocence. But what is this innocence? Certainly it is not ignorance of evil. For no more grisly villains or macabre ogres could be imagined than the wicked queen who bade her henchman bring back Snow White's heart in a casket or the fiendish marionette (Stromboli) and man-eating whale (Monstro) or the wicked Witch of the North and her winged apes. The precise moral and the decided strength of these productions is that in them the world's most patent and potent evil agencies are consigned to their rightfully inferior places and viewed in true perspective against the backdrop of benignity and blessedness. In this respect, innocence consists not so much of freedom from contagion with evil as of a conviction that evil shall not vanquish good, that sin is a temporary aberration, that vice and virtue are plainly opposed, that the former eventually only serves to exercise the latter, that the heart may rise above every sordid circumstance, and that the whole menacing Mystery of Iniquity may be ultimately reduced to a sniveling bogeyman. These are the certainties of an artless mind, an incorruptible, single-eyed outlook that sees God standing in the wings of the universal stage. It is also the mind of the pure of heart and the vowed virgin. As children bask in the sunshine of the assurance that their parents are around to protect them even through thunder and lightning, so the pure of heart see the world, the flesh, and the devil against the background of a smiling God; and their perfect chastity, even as perfect charity, "casts out fear" (1 Jn. 5:18). In innocence thus conceived I think we have the justification of

The Charms of Chastity

the moralist's dictum that one cannot scandalize either the hardened sinner or the confirmed saint.

Looked at from another angle, innocence as a positive quality is akin to an aesthetic aptitude, a sense of beauty. A person who is endowed with an ear for music or an eye for design or a taste for propriety, a person, in short, who has artistic sensibilities, universal or special as it may be, is usually seen to wince or cringe before phenomena grosser constitutions hardly notice, such as cacophonous "music," garish apparel, or mawkish movies. Innocence, I contend, is a sense of moral beauty that makes a person instinctively recoil from the sight of another's sin or the thought of his own surrender to temptation, as if from something deformed and ugly. He glimpses in a flash the disorder and turpitude of, say, physical brutality, sexual license, political corruption, racial inequity, environmental mayhem, or commercial dishonesty; and he is nauseated, though not overwhelmed, at the sight. In the case of Maria Goretti, it was precisely this penchant for the ethically aesthetic, and revulsion from the morally misshapen that infused a martyr's valor into a teenager's heart and eventually ravished the repentant soul of her erstwhile seducer. Conversely, innocence conditions one to relish the spiritual splendor of heroes and heroines great, like the Curé of Ars or Thérèse of Lisieux, and small, like devout old folks

As a white candle in a holy place
Such is the beauty of an aged face

or unspoiled youths

A berry red, a guileless look, a still word—strings of sand!
And yet they made my wild, wild heart fly down
*   to her little hand.*

The third (and most elusive) ingredient of the virtue of chastity is idealism. What I hope to nail down here are two transcendent attitudes that underlie, however subliminally, the profession and practice of chastity. One is the particular vision of romantic love; the other is the universal dream of perfection; both almost defy description. To illustrate this first degree of idealism, let me divulge that, although I am a confirmed bachelor and am amorously detached from every specimen of the fairer sex, I'm head over heels in love with the love-and-marriage ideal and romantically cherish just about the whole of womankind.

To express these sentiments more graphically, I'd like to publicly confess (for the first time in my life) that I broke down and cried when I saw the wind-up of the movie *Marty*, wherein young love blossoms for a balding butcher and a wall-flower schoolmarm. I've been "all choked up" each time I officiated at the wedding of cousins and schoolmates. I own five distinct recordings of *The Desert Song*, an operetta of the twenties that offers a musical commentary on the text: "What therefore God has joined together, let no man put asunder" (Mt. 19:6). And though on occasion (after over-exposure at a Rosary Society Communion Breakfast, or at the fringe of a domestic gab-fest) I could exclaim with Browning,

> *And straight was a path of gold for the sun*
> *And the need of a world of men for me,*

every day is Ladies' Day with me. In young or old, I love their daintiness, their attention to good grooming, their affectivity, their (apparent) helplessness, their personal loyalty, their unmuscularity, their intuition, their persistence, their non-rationality, their idealism—in short, their femininity. I look fondly on the svelte and curvacious maidens bobbing along the sidewalk; I gaze wistfully at stoop-shouldered and dumpy matrons shuffling out of the supermarket. Mine are the bitter-sweet reflections of the singing hay in this Roumanian poem by the Bard of Dimbovitza:

Yesterday's flowers that are yet in me
must needs make way for all tomorrow's flowers.
The maidens, too, that sang me to my death
Must even so make way for all the maids that are to come.
And as my soul, so too their soul will be
Laden with fragrance of days gone by.

Finally, I see the beautiful thing that has grown between my mother, all woman, and my father, every inch a man, after almost fifty years of give-and-take, which is the story of, the glory of, romantic love. I see. I approve. I marvel. But I also see through and beyond. In my heart of hearts I know that this beautiful thing only participates in and but dimly mirrors that "Beauty ever ancient, ever new" which, thanks to the light of grace, I realize may be straightway pursued and oh-so-shortly attained. Almighty God, eventually, is the Sweet Mystery of Life.

We come, at length, to idealism in general. Whatever one thinks of the vow of chastity and the virtue that prompts and protects it, he must admit that those who try to practice perfect chastity do so from idealistic motives—misguided as some see it—and that they are living exponents of a supernatural destiny—however illusory. The practicing idealist may ultimately be proven a fool. But if he is, half of the important words of the language are nonsense, our sweetest lyrics are lies, and every value and virtue and goal is in the long run pointless; for as Browning argued, "A man's reach should exceed his grasp, else what's a Heaven for?"

Implicit in the life of everyone who has willingly chosen perfect chastity is this motive and message: there is a heaven. The very endeavor to reach for the stars in leading a virginal life validates the world's whole lexicon of noble notions: happiness, gladness, ecstasy, fulfillment, harmony, freedom, comfort, peace, fellowship, victory, permanence, certainty, strength, light, life, hope, fidelity, honor, justice, loyalty, mercy, forgiveness, retribution, direction, meaning, significance, purpose, and goal. Because of every living and breathing man and woman of God vowed to chastity, all mankind may be assured in their sometimes faltering convictions about the Kingdom of Heaven, which is variously adumbrated by dozens of *their* most poignant songs. There *is* a long, long trail a-winding, east of the sun and west of the moon, that leads beyond the blue horizon and somewhere over the rainbow, to that land of romance, that cabin in the sky, that castle in the air, and the everlasting toyland that is the New Jerusalem. Thanks to a host of dedicated, full-time followers of the Virgin's Son, our young men will dream dreams and our old men will see visions until all things are made new.

Sponsa Christi

The spouse of Christ for forty years—
A buxom virgin, a doting dame!
Ah, where the dream beneath the heart,
Or beneath the weeds the comely frame?
No lines of toil engrave your face;
No mother's tremors vein your mind.
But you forget those nights you cried,
Your larder of prayers, your obedience blind.

Sweet sister, do not doubt your grace;
Your wimpled face, oh do not despise:
Bespies you through the lattice now
Christ, with ever envious eyes.

9. Super Supper

SUPPOSE SOMEONE broached a busy writer of the high middle ages and asked him what he was working on. Suppose the writer confided, "Oh, I'm planning a poem about hell, purgatory, and heaven." It is not unlikely that curious acquaintance might answer, "Wellll, aren't we *original*! Sounds positively devastating!" Although I'm not Dante and this conference is not exactly a *Divine Comedy*, perhaps my fanciful anecdote may forestall a groan of disappointment on the reader's part when I say that I intend to discuss the Holy Eucharist under three hoary headings: namely, Sacrifice, Sacrament, and Sacred Species. Before launching out into the deep (on this well-charted course), however, I should make a brief apology for my apparently flippant title. At first glance it may seem irreverent to refer to the Eucharist in a Madison Avenue formula, but I insist that the alliterative epithet is accurate and advantageous. It is calculated to evoke pristine astonishment over the *reality* of the Thing and to brush aside from our perspective layers of cobweb-connotations spun by decades of rarified ritual and parochial piety—musty images involving Toomey cassocks, Will and Baumer beeswax, and Benziger Brothers missals. Those who bristle to hear the Eucharist called a Super Supper could be missing the impact of the first revelation, full of mystery and condescension, that Jesus made when he promised the crowds his flesh to eat and his blood to drink.

Super Supper

Super Supper indeed! This is a hard saying, and who can stand it? Yet it is true that the Last Supper, with its manifold cultic implications, is the answer to many yearnings of the human heart. It has proved to be, as they say, a natural . . . or, to stretch the idiom, a *super* natural.

As he reconnoitered human civilization, a visitor from outer space could hardly help being impressed by the multitude, variety, and opulence of religious buildings—as much in evidence in poverty pockets and hinterlands as in sprawling citadels—around the globe: pagodas, tabernacles, mosques, pantheons, basilicas, ziggurats, temples, synagogues, shrines, cathedrals, and revival tents. All these other-worldly structures bear testimony to the world's irresistible instinct (however misguided, in the minds of some) to acknowledge and do homage to a supreme being. Regardless of the size, shape, and furnishings of these (from a natural viewpoint) superfluous and (in both senses) ex-orbitant edifices, they may all be collectively included in just one accurate synonym: they are all "houses of worship." Worship, even to the disinterested eye of an interplanetary observer, should be a phenomenon of prime importance; and the word "worship" bears considerable looking into.

Etymologically, "worship" is an amalgam of two Anglo-Saxon words: *weorth*, meaning worth or value; and *scipe*, a noun-forming suffix that means state, quality, or condition. The suffix was originally added to adjectives (later to nouns as in "friendship") to designate something conspicuous for the quality denoted by the root adjective as in "hard-ship." "Worship," then, means something possessed of exceptional worth. When the word first came into the language it was applied to dignitaries, who were elegantly addressed "Your Worship" (today one speaks to a king as "Your High-ness"). But anything of finite value, a mere king or prince, is almost worthless in comparison to a supreme being. All finite valuables, in fact, shrink to insignificance when stacked up beside what is infinitely priceless. And so in time "worship" came to be applied almost exclusively to the Creator and, eventually, to the act whereby the human heart and mind bow low, figuratively speaking, before the invisible Reality that is all-worthy. In the final analysis, "worship" denotes a religious rite that bespeaks God's worth, a rite of word and gesture (actions speak louder than words) which tells God that he is infinite, or, to put it most simply, a rite which confesses that God is God.

This tortuous venture into the thick woods of Anglo-Saxon etymology may strike the reader as interesting in itself but irrelevant to the discussion of worldwide worship; and he may suspect that I am barking up the wrong tree. But the root meaning of the word "worship" is identical with the basic significance of the religious rites that transpire in every house of worship throughout civilization, whatever the proper word for the rite or the word's derivation. From the beginning men have been going to elaborate lengths to bespeak God's existence and importance. Most often their homage has taken the form of setting aside and annihilating rather valuable possessions, in an attempt to betoken mystically and in miniature how much God means to them. When I first read Homer's *Odyssey*, I was forcibly struck by the piety of hard-bitten, sea-faring pagans many centuries before Christ. At the end of a perilous voyage, Odysseus and his crew routinely poured choice wine into the sand or burnt a fresh carcass on the shore to thank the gods before slaking their thirst or satisfying their hunger. Further readings in history and archeology brought other interesting glimpses into man's efforts at adoration. In their overly zealous devotion, Phoenicians were wont to roast human torsos to honor their deity, Dagon. Under supernatural inspiration the Jews worshipped Yahweh more reasonably than the Phoenicians and more lavishly than the Greeks. It took no small faith for the enterprising Chosen People to stand by and watch herds of prime fillet and droves of grade-A mutton go up in sacrificial smoke on the Temple altars each year.

And yet, if zillions of carcasses, wine-skins, oil-jars, Cadillacs, cyclotrons, metropolises—yes, if the world's gross international output were smashed into atoms on one cosmic altar, man would not begin to worship God properly: God is infinite; men and all their goods and chattel are finite. Even the God-inspired sacrifices of Abel and Abraham, of Melchisedech and Moses, though offered with deep reverence, were *essentially* worthless as tokens of God's worth. It is radically impossible for man to worship God adequately . . . unless . . . unless the offering be priceless. When in the upper room Jesus whispered over elemental bread and wine, "This is my body . . . this is my blood," thereby anticipating and memorializing his sacrifice on the cross, a man fulfilled for the first time and once and for all the very purpose of creation: he adequately showed forth, he eloquently bespoke the true worth of Almighty God. This parity between the act and the object of worship can be verified throughout the New Testament. It will suffice here to see Saint Paul's explanation to the Philippians: "His state was divine, yet he did not cling to his equality with God but emptied himself to assume the condition of a slave, and became as men are; and being as all men are, he was humbler yet, even to accepting death, death on a cross" (2:6-9).

So far we have been discussing the nature and, as it were, quantity of worship. It is time now to qualify Christ's worship and to provide a further rationale for his sacrifice. If worship involves declaring God's worth, an accomplishment only a God-man is equal to, then sin, an activity all mankind seems proficient at, is in its essence the very antithesis of worship. Disobeying God's law is tantamount to denying his dominion and, ultimately, his divinity. Therefore, to all practical purposes, man's worship of God, historically and not just theoretically considered, has to take the shape of canceling out the denial of God that sin implies and must, first and foremost, be propitiatory worship. Thereafter and secondarily worship may embrace the other "ends of prayer" such as thanksgiving, petition, and praise (all of these implicitly and simultaneously declare God's dominion and worth). The act of worship, then, *must be* some form of mortification, executed with contrition for conciliatory purposes. Hence Christ's sanguine sacrifice, his mortal immolation: "For it has pleased the Father that in him all his fullness should dwell, and that through him he should reconcile to himself all things, whether on earth or in the heavens, making peace by the blood of the cross" (Col. 1:19-20).

Unquestionably, Christ's sacrificial death was, objectively speaking, the perfect, the appropriate act of worship. And that sacrifice is over and done . . . it is consummated. But it is likewise obvious that men do not cease to need to express themselves to God, subjectively speaking, not only in repentance over their on-going sins but also out of the promptings of gratitude, dependence, and awe, as occasion dictates. In instituting the Last Supper, Jesus left us the means to re-enact his bloody sacrifice, not just in symbol but even in reality. By virtue of sacramental reality, however mysterious it may seem, the Sacrifice of the Mass is both a representation and a re-presentation of Calvary; and through the Mass men may personally satisfy all their religious instincts. Saint Paul's first letter to the Corinthians is explicit and emphatic about the ontological reality of the ritual celebration of Christ's sacrifice on the cross: "For this is what I received from the Lord, and in turn pass on to you: that on the same night that he was betrayed, the Lord Jesus took some bread and thanked God for it and broke it, and he said, 'This is my body, which is for you; do this as a memorial of me.' In the same way he took the cup after supper and said, 'This cup is the new covenant in my blood. Whenever you drink it, do

Super Supper

this as a memorial of me.' Until the Lord comes, therefore, every time you eat this bread and drink this cup, you are proclaiming his death" (1 Cor. 11:23-27). Space does not allow me to develop further the first and most important aspect of Christ's Super Supper. To fully appreciate the centrality of this meal-sacrifice ritual, one should research the significance of the Passover ceremony, which looms large in the Jewish consciousness, as well as study the succinct but dramatic Institution passages in the Synoptics and the solemn and detailed promise of the ritual in Saint John's sixth chapter.

It should now be clear that, regardless of the profusion, diversity, and magnificence of the world's houses of worship, only upon the altars in Catholic churches is the Mass offered from the rising of the sun to the setting thereof; and so her buildings alone, strictly speaking, qualify as houses of worship. When minister and congregation meet, moreover, the essential religious service that takes place does not consist in catechetics or sacred oratory, vocal prayers or chanted hymns, felt fervor or psychological excitement, but it lies in the performance ("liturgy" is the Greek word for action) of an ancient act that proclaims, unconditionally and unassailably, the death of the Lord until he comes. This is not to say that the priest and people need not "get into the act" by personally echoing the Savior's sentiments and appropriately imitating his corporeal sacrifice: "Think of God's mercy, my brothers, and worship him, I beg you, in a way worthy of thinking beings, by offering your living bodies as a holy sacrifice, truly pleasing to God. Do not model yourselves on the behavior of the world around you, but let your behavior change, modeled by your new mind" (Rom. 12:1-2).

Probably the most powerful instrument worshippers have to help conform their morals and mentality to the Lord's is Holy Communion. The sacramental body and blood which is confected and distributed during Mass is a sort of sublime K-ration for the members of the Church Militant, enabling them to cope with life and to personally conquer the world, the flesh, and the devil. That spiritual succor for the individual Christian (not the symbolizing of congregational unity) is the over-riding function of Holy Communion is obvious from the words of Jesus' promise: "I am the living bread which has come down from heaven. Anyone who eats this bread will live forever; and the bread that I shall give is my flesh, for the life of the world . . . . For my flesh is real food and my blood is real drink. He who eats my flesh and drinks my blood lives in me and I live in him" (Jn. 6:51, 55-56). Reams could be written on the scriptural prototypes of this celestial nourishment (the unleavened bread, the manna in the desert, the loaves of proposition, Elijah's heaven-sent food, Elisha's multiplication of bread, and, of course, Christ's wine and bread miracles); and pages could be piled in historical testimony to the power of the sacrament. Here I wish only to speak briefly about the mechanics of Communion and the dispositions of the communicant.

Unlike other nourishment, which is absorbed by and assimilated into the partaker, this sacramental food, under ideal conditions, gradually transforms the recipient into the food—into Jesus Christ—not only morally into his "spirit" but ontologically into his Mystical Body. The parallel between physical nourishment and Holy Communion is only partial. But the pure notion of union or identification, which underlies the food metaphor is borne out completely. God's loving union with man and man's loving union with God could not be better expressed or effected than by God coming so close to man as to enter him and by man coming so near to God as to get inside him (Christ's Mystical Body). A secondary unity, naturally, springs from the Eucharist: unity among the communicants. As they approach God, they breach the gap between one another.

Super Supper

The beneficent operation of Holy Communion takes place objectively and automatically every time one who is conscious of no mortal guilt receives the Sacrament. Call the phenomenon magic, but it is white magic, of a piece with God's first gratuitous call to justification and unmerited invitations to repentance. If the faithful are without serious sin, it is an incalculable advantage for them to partake of the Eucharist no matter how undevout they feel or unappreciative they may be. Doubtless, the full power of the Sacrament depends upon the communicant's optimum intention and attention. But Communion essentially "works" even when the communicant minimally cooperates. Another reading of John's sixth chapter will convince the faint-hearted, moreover, that the boon of Christ's body and blood is intended as a crutch for the weak, not a reward for the virtuous. No one should hesitate to heed our Savior's summons in the most pragmatic way possible by receiving Holy Communion often: "Come to me, all you who labor and are burdened, and I will refresh you" (Mt. 11:28).

We come, at length, to the last feature of the Super Supper: the abiding presence of Jesus, Emmanuel (Hebrew for "God is with us"). There is a peculiar furnishing in Catholic churches missing from other houses of worship—that gold-plated breadbox containing the Sacred Species. To illustrate the marvel of the Lord's sacramental presence, whereby he makes good the consoling promise of his Ascension ("Behold, I am with you all days, even to the end of time"), I would like to explain the tabernacle by drawing three fanciful analogies, likening it to a television set, a medicine chest, and a window in the wall of the world.

Not long ago I watched the motion picture Grand Hotel and thrilled to see before my very eyes events unfold that were filmed a year before my birth. And the thought occurred that it was but an arbitrary quirk of history that the "talkies" had been perfected only by the twentieth century. Is it so unthinkable that motion pictures and television had been developed by some genius in antiquity like Archimedes? The Greek scientist, who lived two hundred years B.C., envisioned a lever long enough to jostle the earth. Given auspicious conditions, could he not have televised contemporary events and beamed them to some distant tele-star, and might we of the twentieth century not receive the relay broadcast today? These musings are mere wishful thinking. But if you stop and consider that, according to Catholic doctrine, Jesus is really, truly, and substantially present in the Blessed Sacrament and that, in the words of the Epistle to the Hebrews, Jesus is "the same yesterday, today, yes, and forever" (13:8) then you may concede that the whole of his life lies before you in the tabernacle. You have only to switch on the current of a lively faith, and YOU ARE THERE; you can witness at will any episode in the continuing drama of The Greatest Story Ever Told. Your meditations before the tabernacle on the original Christmas, your mental replay of the sermon on the mount, your contemplation on the passion and death will not be wishful thinking. For time and space categories collapse when the object of your reflections is an infinite Person sacramentally present.

The tabernacle is also a medicine chest, from which the Divine Physician administers grace to heal and strengthen our souls. The woman in Capernaum who suffered from constant hemorrhage simply brushed the hem of Christ's robe, and healing power "went out from him" (Lk. 8:44). If anyone comes into the presence of the Eucharist and with belief begs for help, he will experience the Lord's curative ministrations. He has salve to soothe the throbbing conscience and drops to clear the clouded mind. He has antidotes to cool the fever of concupiscence and tonics to stimulate the paralyzed will. Whatever the complaint, however complicated the problem, a visit to the Blessed Sacrament will bring immediate relief. A sophisticated intellectual, Saint Thomas Aquinas used to rest his head on the tabernacle when beset with doctrinal perplexities and found solutions. No one should feel squeamish about taking his troubles to the chapel, to the medicine chest of the tabernacle.

Msgr. Ronald Knox saw the tabernacle as a window in the wall of the world, and so it is. I saw a remarkable sketch once hanging on the wall of a seminarian's bedroom. It was a view looking out through the tabernacle into a church lined with empty pews. Such is the scene Jesus has habitually beheld throughout the centuries in his sacramental presence. But whenever someone drops in to visit the tabernacle, the Lord's vista is greatly expanded. He can see the visitor and see through him, see his past, present, and future. For now the person may be overflowing with fervor or numb of heart, but Jesus can foresee him committing sin in a wanton moment and anticipate an inconspicuous act of kindness. He can fondly recall the visitor in his First Communion clothes and remember him lisping his penance after confession. All patience, Jesus never turns a deaf ear or withholds his consolation. Jesus longs to see him one day, not darkly as in glass, but face to face on the other side of the world, where dwells the Lord with the heroes and heroines of all times. Thanks to the Sacred Species then, our happiness lies right under our eyes; and the Kingdom of God is in our midst wherever there stands a Catholic house of worship.

No commentary on the Super Supper, with its trinity of marvels, would be complete if it failed to note that this recurring ritual is also a preview of coming attractions and a rehearsal of the everlasting reunion-banquet of heaven. Then, in unspeakable conviviality, the saints will feast their eyes on the Beatific Vision and never know satiety. Everything, finally, that I have tried to say in this conference is nicely summed up in a venerable ejaculation taught us in the noviatiate:

> *O sacred Banquet*
> *in which Christ is eaten*
> *His Passion is recalled,*
> *the soul is filled with grace*
> *And a pledge of future glory*
> *is given to us.*

So Also For Himself

Now is the yellow, unctious month of May,
And my Ordination lies but a week away.
Red-rubric chains have twined my mind and hands;
A hundred mock Masses locked these loving bands.
To lesser Levites from whom I soon must sever
My clean cards went: "Thou art a priest forever."
To former friends I sent gay invitations,
Announcing a newest Aaron's first celebrations.
Alas, when all flowers and firstfruits are out,
Shall I forget the former sin, the doubt;
Shall there not be, as there has been, the stain,
Once sacred oils dissolve the swathes in twain?

But then the prince-priest, before his Mass began,
Yelled one night, "I do not know the Man!"

10. *Last Things First*

IF MEMORY SERVES me right, it was Bishop Sheen who recounted the following exchange with his teenage nephew. At a propitious moment Sheen casually inquired, "Tom, what are you going to do with the rest of your life?" Without a moment's hesitation the nephew answered, "Why, I'm going to attend a good liberal arts college and then enter medical school." "And what do you plan to do next?" Uncle Fulton queried further. "Well, I suppose I'll work in a hospital for a while and learn the profession inside out." "And then what, Tom?" "Then I'd like to move to a rural area and become a general practitioner." "That's fine," the uncle agreed, but he would not leave off his cross-examination: "Then what do you propose to do?" The boy speculated a moment and confessed, "If all goes well, I'll build up a good practice, deliver a lot of babies, and graciously retire when my replacement arrives." Still with raised eyebrow, the uncle prodded, "And then?" "After that . . . after that . . . well, I hope to play a lot of golf, visit my children, and fool around with my grandchildren." The bothersome bishop would not relent: "Then?" "Gee whiz! Uncle, then I'll be pushing up daisies—what do you think I'll be doing?" blurted the boy in exasperation, thinking he was off the hook at last. "And just what do you plan to do then—for all eternity?" Sheen asked with a knowing smile. For once the lad was speechless. Never before had he been brought face to face so dramatically and so unsuspectingly with the thought of ultimate reality. After this encounter, so the bishop claims, Tom continued

Last Things First

to plan his career in detail and to ask help from his guidance counsellor at school; but he began to view those precarious plans and that mundane advice in the white light of his eternal destiny. Thanks to his wily uncle, Tom learned early in life the wisdom of putting last things first.

At this time of the ecclesiastical year, the Church bids all her children remember their last end in the hope that the sobering recollection of death, Judgment, Hell, and Heaven will inspire them to amend their lives and to stir up the grace that is in them—all this, as a preparation for the festival of the Incarnation. Speaking for myself, I have always found the subjects of death, Judgment, Hell, and Heaven not just sobering and salutary but even exciting and consoling. In this last conference, then, I would like to put last things first and to muse briefly on these four finalities (as well as the transitory eschatological stage known as Purgatory). The topic of Heaven will get (and deserve) the lion's share of my attention. But apart from this emphasis, this conference may resemble a miniature *Divine Comedy* (assuming, optimistically, that it does not simply prove to be *Father Robert's Follies*). In any event, on with the show!

Like mothers-in-law, death is a phenomenon at once unavoidable and inscrutable, serious and comical. Chesterton, I think, has somewhere treated of the mystical side of mothers-in-law; and some day I hope to explore, from a purely natural point of view, the bizarre character of earthly departure. Here I want to examine death only from a theological viewpoint. And from such a viewpoint, the first thing to be noted about death is that it is hardly a theological subject. I mean that, despite the fact that asceticism and the skull-and-crossbones have been somewhat fused in the Christian imagination and regardless of the fact that a "talk on death" was for a long time standard fare in the parish mission or the religious retreat, when you come right down to it, man's mortality is not exactly an object of Revelation or a part of the *depositum fidei*, or even a paramount theme in Sacred Scripture. Death is as certain as taxes, and just as secular.

In fact the pagans of ancient Greece and Rome were considerably more obsessed with man's mortality, and heathens such as the Vikings and Iroquois were far more elaborate in their obsequies than Christians ever were (prescinding from the twentieth-century North American variety): further proof that at least the first of the "last things" is not a central item in our Creed. That is why I have always been a bit wary about priests who harp on death from the pulpit. One of the few tolerably good preachers in my hometown parish (which shall go unnamed) happened to be related to me, so I do not think he will mind my telling this story on him as he looks down from heaven. Forceful as Father Lally admittedly was, the invariable motif of all his sermons was—you guessed it—death. And sure enough, each passing week in the parish would bring fresh relevance to his theme as one more senior parishioner went through life's thin ice. But I feel that all of Father Lally's crossbones rattling was neither doctrinally *de rigeur* nor an adequate measure of his metier. And to this day I do not know if my uncle's brother the priest was aware of his ludicrous knickname throughout the diocese: "Death Valley" Lally.

Granting, then, that the preacher can exaggerate the gravity of the graveyard, I do think, nevertheless, that every man should occasionally indulge in funereal considerations. It should not unhinge a grown man's mind to walk actually or imaginatively through a graveyard and ponder over the brevity of life and reckon the whole cities of the dead that lie still beneath civilization's feverish tread. It should be galvanizing, not paralyzing, to reflect now and then on the certainty of one's own death and the uncertainty of the attendant circumstances thereof. But it is also true enough that the recurring images of black hearses and gray headstones can have a depressing effect—almost psychosomatic—on one's psyche; and if only to relieve the believer of that pressure, I offer the following fanciful consideration.

My mother's younger sister was the last of a rapid-fire succession of relatives I helped usher out of this world with the consoling rites of Christian burial. Aunt Gertrude died about the same time the astronauts had encircled the moon; and as I glimpsed her metallic gray coffin in the center aisle, I was struck with a bracing insight which I have not ceased to capitalize on in my Requiem Mass homily. The casket was a space capsule; the catafalque was the launching pad, and the Requiem Service was the countdown. We were actually shooting Aunt Gertrude into outer space: it only *looked* as if we were planting her remains in the earth (like a giant seed). Further exploration of this analogy reminded me that Jesus was the first astronaut, in view of his Ascension; and Mary was the first woman in space by virtue of her Assumption. Then it dawned on me that we were not dispatching Gertrude into outer space: we were sending her back to earth, that is, back to her real home, back to Heaven. We here on *terra firma* were in fact the real travelers in outer space. We were the pilgrims, the wayfarers; the planet was an out-sized rocketship. Aunt Gertrude was winging her way swiftly back to the jubilant throngs gathered in New Jerusalem Square, awaiting her homecoming. Why, the death of a believing Christian is, ultimately, no more macabre than Dorothy's abrupt departure from Munchkin Land and prompt return to the arms of loving friends and relations in Kansas.

Even if Christians are not supposed to sorrow "as the heathen do," they do feel, as do survivors in every religious persuasion, beholden to and solicitous for the dear departed. To despise, deny, or belittle this instinctive concern and thoroughly human altruism would be unrealistic or supercilious. Though the generality of mankind yearn to do something for the deceased, the Roman Catholic Church alone (that is, not including even the Orthodox "branches") teaches that survivors can offer salutary good works and prayers for the dead. True, the doctrine of Purgatory has rather scant support from Scripture, but immemorial Christian tradition and every rational consideration commend to us the existence of an ante-chamber to Paradise—and there are those clear exhortations from Maccabees II, to pray and give alms in behalf of the faithful departed. This mutual trust, as it were, of suffrages and sufferings is but an eschatological extension of a much more presently popular doctrine of the Mystical Body. Many of our separated brothers suspect that this peculiarly Roman Catholic construct, Purgatory, is as gratuitous and imaginary as the limbo of the unbaptized; but, then, they are not usually inclined to concede the principle that tradition as well as Scripture is a channel of Revelation, nor are most of them adept at making fine theological distinctions. A more serious objection to the doctrine of Purgatory stems from their belief that anything less than instant and unconditional salvation upon conversion would derogate from the efficacy of the Savior's redeeming grace: conversion, salvation, and blessedness are all attributable, one hundred percent, to Jesus, so they contend. But deep in their hearts these good Christians know that they can "fill up in their bodies" what is lacking in the sufferings of Christ; they realize in their bones that they can merit crowns of variable size and that "star differeth from star" in the resurrection, and they are thoroughly convinced of the completely social character of Christianity. In fine, they really, if implicitly, believe in the doctrine of Purgatory.

Having jumped from the graveyard to the subject of Purgatory, I am guilty of violating chronological order—if, strictly speaking, there be a chronological order at all in the afterlife. I did neglect to treat of the very sentence that consigned the lucky soul to Purgatory. (Such a one *is* lucky: read Cardinal Newman's *Dream of Gerontius* to see how happily a Heaven-bound citizen faces Purgatory's Hell-like but terminal punishments.) The only insight that I wish to impart about the Particular Judgment is simply to show that when God judges the individual soul, it is not so much that he softens his justice with mercy as it is that his judgment is so just, it is merciful: the whole truth and nothing but the truth is the merciful truth. Here in *this* conference, at least, there is no need for me to enlarge upon the General Judgment; for I am more or less concerned with following the path of an individual (hypothetical) soul. The thrilling impact following upon that moment of truth which the Particular Judgment constitutes will be magnified and multiplied a zillion-fold on that longest day when all flesh shall reveal and reflect upon the mercy and justice that meet and kiss in God's cosmic Providence.

But regarding the Particular Judgment, I will say that this event should hold in store for the greater preponderance of humanity an exciting and welcome prospect, rather than the expectation of nameless doom and dread. For mankind by and large does hunger and thirst for justice and is delighted by every well-executed judgment in creative literature. Theater literature abounds with award-winning courtroom drama: *Twelve Angry Men*, *A Reasonable Doubt*, *Johnny Belinda*, to name a few titles. Add to these the welter of crime detection movies and television lawyer perennials such as *Perry Mason*, *Judd for the Defense*, *The Bold Ones*, and *The Defenders*; and you begin to realize that we mortals are pretty much preoccupied with the meting out of justice. If most of us find a satisfying catharsis in witnessing the vicarious uncovering of guilt and innocence, the drama-turgic deliverance of deserved comeuppances, the verisimilitude reward of secret virtue, or the fictive punishment of unmasked villany—then most of us will surely find it an electrifying experience to attend the eschatological version of *This Is Your Life*, with our divine Master as master of ceremonies and each of us surprised earthlings as guest of honor. For most of us well-intentioned souls in all likelihood let the memory of little kindnesses, of long-haul patience, of instinctive forbearance, and of other moments with our best foot unconsciously forward go clean out of our mind. Oh, the record of our cowardly compromises and selfish indulgence will not be swept under the celestial rug, either But we will regret these lapses not with the limp and facile remorse of self-disappointment but with the overpowering, bitter-sweet repentance over falling so far short of God's all encompassing, ingenious love—now manifested in this feast of forgiveness. In that hour—I speak, of course, for men of good will—in that hour one's heart will glow within him, as it did for the disciples whom Jesus encountered on the way to Emmaus, when one realizes how intimately Providence had been entwined with the strands of his life, how proximately God had viewed the hills and vales of life's itinerary, and how fondly the Holy Spirit had brooded over and nurtured one's growth in prayer and grace. Our Particular Judgment, then, will be our moment of truth *par excellence*; and that truth, like no other, will set us free.

Since even before the papacy of John XXIII, there seems to have been a gentlemen's agreement among preachers in Holy Mother Church not to say a mumbling word about Hell. Maybe—after the horrors of Auschwitz and Buchenwald, the cold-war threat of nuclear holocausts, and the cold-blooded brutalities of little Third-World wars—maybe we mortals did not need oratorical reminders of Hell's imminence just at the time. But I for one cannot ignore or minimize eternal punishment until the Holy Father directs us to tear out whole pages of the Good News as being typographical errors (ascribable, no doubt, to some clumsy printer's devil). No, the Good Shepherd did not mince words about the everlasting garbage heap (Gehenna), whence not even he could rescue the errant lamb. However, since the present generation still appears to be constantly tottering on the edge of neurosis, there is no need to focus long or closely on the features of the Inferno. I shall simply suggest that we might deduce for ourselves some of the frightful conditions of the underworld environment by considering the qualities of glorified bodies in reverse.

While studying the theology of the Resurrection as a seminarian, I learned that the resurrected body would be characterized by four glorious qualities—attributes which the risen Christ seems to have displayed during his forty-day sojourn with his disciples before ascending into Heaven: agility, or the power to transport oneself anywhere in the world instantly (to move through closed doors and to dartle between Capernaum and Jerusalem in the twinkling of an eye); impassibility, or the incapacity of feeling pain—nail wounds, thorn pricks, spear jabs; subtilty, or independence from physical susceptibilities such as hunger, thirst, weariness; and finally, glory, or the emission of an observable radiance from the then-perfected body. Such shall be the features, theologians (used to) tell us, of physical life for those who arise to salvation. The situation for those who arise to damnation, it would seem, will prove quite the contrary. Immobility will be their lot; they cannot stir from the infernal regions; some may even have their heads, as Dante envisioned it, forever stuck in unyielding ice. Instead of an uncanny insensitivity to pain, the Hell-dweller will bear about in his body a preternatural supersensitivity to pain—probably to some appropriate traumatic stimulus. Rather than being independent from the demands of the body, each lost soul will be taunted and tantalized by unfulfilled, unfulfillable appetites—very likely in accordance with their peculiar sins of the flesh. Finally, in place of the irradiating glory associated with the saints, the damned will be bathed in the ghastly, flickering strobe lights of Hell fire. Saint Augustine, ex-sinner though he was, made short shrift with the geography of Hell, so I may be pardoned if I scant the topography of its tortures: it is as easy to overdo them as it is to burn a steak. The important question regarding the nether world is not where it is or what it is like, but, as the Bishop of Hippo was wont to point out, how to escape going there.

Just about the nicest way to escape Hell is to think long and hard enough about Heaven, as did Saint Francis of Assisi, for whom the mere whisper of the word occasioned a rapture. We have it on no less an authority than Sacred Scripture that the blessedness of Heaven transcends the powers of human imagination and beggars all description. Yet one would think that our best poets and word-mongers, not to mention the philosophers and theologians, might have more frequently and strenuously essayed the subject of Heaven, a matter so huge in importance and rich in suggestion. Of course, I am prescinding here in my strictures from utopian literature—which stretches from Plato's *Republic* and More's *Utopia* to Butler's *Erewhon* and Huxley's *Brave New World*—for these and kindred works are satiric swipes at real society rather than serious delineations of an ideal state; and besides, their authors' imaginative sights were leveled at the considerably lower target of an earthly paradise. As for the details of a celestial Paradise, off the top of my head, I can think of a mere handful of literary attempts at articulation, and these derive heavily from the two dominant images of Scripture, that is, the endless feast and the hosanna-singing chorus: Dante's *Paradiso*, parts of Milton's *Paradise Lost*, Maeterlinck's *The Bluebird* (one scene of it), Shaw's *Don Juan in Hell* (the roué's version of Heaven), and Marc Connelly's *Green Pastures*. It is this last-mentioned interpretation of celestial beatitude that, for all its grotesquerie, impresses me as being the warmest, most credible, and most complete account of what Heaven will be like.

Connelly's play, you will remember, opens with a Negro

Baptist minister conducting a Sunday School class down South. As the avuncular reverend proceeds to answer a young fidgeting skeptic's riddles about the supernatural, the scene gives way to a bustling fishfry in some Dixie woodland. Ambling about and supervising the fishing and the frying and the feasting is the Lord God, a six-foot-four Nubian in stove hat and coat of tails; wherever he moves the Lord is shadowed by his right-hand man, Gabriel, a carbon copy of Jack Benny's valet Rochester, who is forever proffering his Boss a genu-wine five-cent ceegar. Whatever problems threaten in the course of the picnic, the Lord instantly irons out—making the catfish bite, sending the cumulonimbuses scudding off, and patching up quarrels among some pickaninnies. Everyone is on the whole full of bliss, and the greatest happiness of all is just being with and talking to the Lord. Now, to some students of eschatology, this cotton-picker's conception of Heaven may appear a little less gross than the Koran's technicolor previews of coming attractions—a Paradise of lush hanging gardens, curvaceous houris, fragrance of spikenard, and decanters of nectar. It would be forward of me, I know, to ask what is so wrong with the Mohammedan Heaven; but I *will* say that the faithful do need a concrete and stimulating image of beatitude, no matter how sublime or subtle Heaven's joys may prove, if we saints (with a small s) are to approach anywhere near the motivation which drove the Saints to heroic measures for the sake of the Kingdom. I contend that the foregoing black cameo version of the New Jerusalem, even if it is not to every believer's eschatological taste, can show us the way to envisage our Heavenly destiny realistically and compellingly.

For some reasonable analysis, with some assist from revelation, it seems that the blessedness of Heaven is comprised of four distinct causes of joy—all of which are graphically adumbrated in Connelly's drama. Thus, we can understand that in Heaven discomfort is no more; everyone is at rest (or better, at home); all are comrades; and God unbares his goodness, truth, and beauty . . . and is infinitely nice to be near.

Freedom from want and hurt seems to me to be, logically, the first bliss of Heaven. In the New Jerusalem every tear will be wiped away, and there will be no more sighing or groaning; for all these former disagreeable things shall have passed away. As at the pickaninnies' picnic, the sun will ever shine; the glass will stand at a comfortable height; and no one will be inclined to cuss the humidity. But just think of a few more implications under the heading of this first joy of Heaven; broaden the horizon of the happiness in the offing on this one score alone. No more tears—yes, and no more heart attacks or heart aches, no more cancers or cankers, no more drudgery or ennui, no more whip-cracking or wise-cracking, no more insignificance or over-exposure, no more left-overs or hand-me-downs, no more odious comparisons or body odor, no more mortgages or leaking mufflers, no more mosquitoes or coffee grounds, no more hangovers or hiccups, no more role-playing and being on parole, no more dwarfs and wallflowers, no more tanks and floods, no more small pox and small talk, no more pecking order and pimples, no more insomnia and drug nods, no more malnutrition and sunburn, no more elephantiasis and failing grades, no more rubber bullets and moth holes, no more pink-eye and red-eye, no more fish bones and loan sharks, no more sales taxes and emphysema, no more hi-fi flutter and prostitution, no more earthquakes and fallen cakes, no more tracheotomies and railroad strikes, no more thunder and napalm, no more skyjacking and obesity, no more meetings and club dues, no more child-beating and cribbing, no more night court and crop-burning, no more baldness and harelip, no more overdue fines and bifocals, no more strontium 90 fallout and thalidomide babies, no more spinsterhood and black-widow spiders, no more Olympic shoot-outs and common colds, no more deadlines and bread lines, no more getting up on cold mornings and rainy vacations, no more two-star movies and colliding oilers, no more being fired and hangnails, no more money-mad pastors and phoney gurus. You can try your own hand at this litany of "former things" that shall, hopefully, have passed away. If your imagination falters, simply consult your nearest newspaper for suggestions as to what sub-lunar liabilities will be conspicuous by their absence up yonder.

The next degree of joy in Heaven is more positive. Call it finding fulfillment, coming to rest, being at peace . . . arriving home. Whatever the precise character or personal tone of this kind of beatitude, I feel certain that it will not be something utterly exotic and adventitious. I have an intuition that if this joy may be likened to the excitement of finding and getting a pearl of great price, it will be thrice as thrilling inasmuch as the discovery is made in one's own back yard as it were. To express the idea another way, I feel that we will not experience this degree of bliss by crossing over the rainbow and laying hands on a pot of celestial gold, but rather we will shed the scales from our eyes and see that we have been basking in rainbow light and sitting amidst gold. In a word, we will find the here and now apotheosized; the apocalypse, like beauty, is in the eye of the beholder. Words would certainly fail me if I tried to pinpoint this happiness further—that is, if I tried directly to describe it. But I do think I can convey some inkling of the nature of this joy by explaining that it shall be an amalgam of all the satisfactions novelists and playwrights and script writers have striven to inject into the denouements of their slice-of-life opuses.

For example, off hand I think of Ebenezer Scrooge's resurrected *joie de vivre* that prompted him to send the urchin off to fetch from the butcher shop a goose as big as the boy. Then there is Jody's bittersweet emergence from the rites of initiation when he returns the yearling deer to the Florida wilds; or the lighter but still heart-tugging joy of

Junior Miss when Peggy Ann Garner sheds bobby socks and braces. Add to this fulfillment Tom Cortney's successful matriculation at a Scots med school with the help of a bequest from doughty old Charles Coburn in the film version of Cronin's *The Green Years*. Or take what appears a seamier but is really a richer, more redemptive finale: the fittingness of Burton's decision to stay on with the unmoored widow Ava Gardner in *The Night of the Iguana*. If that joy seems too dubious, balance it off with the sprightly, heart-warming denouement of Tennessee Williams's madcap matrimonial comedy *A Period of Adjustment*. To glimpse the quality and intensity of the second bliss of Heaven I am trying to illuminate, the reader must imagine these and all other fictional happy endings piled on top of each other. But that is not all; for all these instances of fulfillment are extraneous to him—they are merely parallels or paradigms of that special, that personal apotheosis which will be his alone. Speaking for myself again, if I should achieve Heaven, there my peculiar (in both senses of the word) my peculiar dreams will take shape for me; my visions will materialize. I really believe that the positive premium to which I allude, this second bliss of Heaven, will fit like an old belt, will be a grand finale which, though indescribable and unimaginable, I should have suspected all along. Those "many mansions" will actually feel like home sweet home.

Certainly one of the least mysterious of the great expectations Heaven holds out for us is the third beatitude—that of being re-united with loved ones, of befriending one's heroes, and of making precious acquaintances. In the world of the newspaper, it is a well-known fact that the most widely read columns, the newspaper's staple selling point, are the human interest columns; the society page, the personality-parade section, the names-in-the-news box. For the paramount interest of people by and large is people at large. That is why the prospect of joining the citizenry of the New Jerusalem, it seems to me, provides the roundest, most realistic, most cogent reason for resisting evil and doing good in a pinch or over the long haul. In fact, just the other day I was explaining to a benign atheist the honest, unofficial argument I propound to prove to myself God's existence. My private apology for theism might shame a gorilla or make Saint Thomas turn over in his grave, but it certainly prods me into refusing to accept ancestry from the apes, even as it convinces me utterly and irrevocably of life beyond the grave. You see, Uncle Jack was a good, fun-loving, fun-making man who came nowhere near being fulfilled in this life. Slight of build, he was a classic specimen of the childless, hen-pecked husband. This good little guy, who never ceased to bring us nephews the bits of small treasures fallen out of anonymous pockets at the dry-cleaning plant where he toiled for twenty years—jacknives, hankies, watch-fobs—this little guy who occasionally took a wee drop too much and got clobbered by my mother's sister, this guy who joked rain or shine about how his company was cleaning up in the dyeing business but dying in the cleaning business, this little guy had to be imperishable—had to be living on and on in perpetual jollity, richly rewarded for all the slings and arrows of outrageous fortune he had borne in his mortal flesh. Granting an Uncle Jack, I knew in my heart of hearts there had to be a Great Washing Day and A Dry-Cleaning Plant in the Sky.

Yes, we should all think often and seriously about the hope of rejoining good and faithful kith and kin in the Hereafter. Unquestionably, I expect to meet my ten top heroes in Heaven: Jesus, Chesterton, Saint Francis, Gerard Manley Hopkins, Cardinal Newman, Danny Kaye, Nelson Eddy, Victor Herbert, Franz Lehar, and Basil Rathbone. I do look forward to comparing notes with the Twelve Apostles, Houdini, Saint Thérèse, and Jane Austen. But my knowledge of these folks is purely professional or intellectual. The people I viscerally miss here below and yearn to revisit with eternally up above are my departed relatives and friends—Grampa, my Irish grandfather who took his tomatoes with sugar on them; Aunt Mollie, who used to deal the cards when the family played penny-ante into the wee, small hours; Buddy Taylor, who used to live upstairs and was lost in a submarine during World War II; Ben and Bill, for thirty-five years the proprietors of our little red-brick candy store; Norman Van Ness, the wonderful artist and clarinetist who graduated from high school with me and died a year later while serving in the Air Corps Band . . . . These are just a few typical souls that I hope and expect to be reunited with if I lead a good life here on earth, stay humble, and lean on God's arm a lot.

At last we come to the fourth beatitude of Heaven, seeing God face to face. So difficult is it to put into words just what joys the Beatific Vision involves, that some intellectual snobs such as G. B. Shaw and Mark Twain have rashly concluded that the whole idea is so much bilgewater, and they have lampooned the Heavenly hosts that gaze unblinkingly on the Divine Graybeard. Shaw, for example, has his Don Juan liken the activity of intuiting God to attending an endless, insufferably boring Sunday afternoon concert or theosophy lecture. Quite at home in Hell, the witty rogue claims that he would find the pleasures of Heaven so starchy and stifling that life down below was infinitely preferable. If he was being serious, Shaw should have known better.

I will wager Shaw did not find his adorable Wagnerian operas tedious or intolerable. Well, gazing on God, I like to think, will be better and more exciting than watching a never-ending, never-palling, three-dimension, stereophonic, technicolor, panavision, star-studded, five-star, budget-unlimited, shot-on-location, drama-musical extravaganza. It will be so absorbing, no one will leave for popcorn or coke, and aeons will slip by without notice. "Lord, it is good for us to be here," will be our unvarying response. And, oddly enough, we will not be mere idle spectators; somehow, we will be swept up into the production and get into the act. It will be a cosmic happening more than a spectacle: happiness will be happening, now and ever after. The beauty behind every beauty—Gershwin's syncopation, Nicklaus's follow-through, Shakespeare's high bombast, Bjoerling's high C, Rubens's burnt gold; the truth behind all truth—the Periodic Table, the Library of Congress, Grimm's Law, the Theory of Relativity, Topology, Etymology, Endocrinology; the goodness behind all goodness—martyrdom, patience, generosity, altruism, diligence, forbearance, solicitude, innocence, loyalty: all these but darkly intimate the kaleidoscopic riches that lie within the unplummetable vortex of Divine Being.

When all is said and done, my efforts at suggesting what the joys of Heaven may be like must prove utterly unequal to the task. Saint Paul has said the last, most pregnant (if most laconic) thing about the last of the Four Last Things: "Eye has not seen, nor ear heard, nor has it entered the heart of man what good things God has prepared for those who love Him." Nevertheless, in the light of this faltering conference, I hope and pray that a few more of the faithful are dying to get to Heaven.

A Most Ingenious Paradox

I bound my eyes and shut my ears
In penance. I preferred
What eye hath never seen before,
Nor ear hath ever heard.

I parched my tongue and tamed my taste
To hold in higher favor
The water welling, never failing,
The Bread of deathless savor.

I locked my hands and crooked my knees
That one day I might greet
Jesus, wounded hand in hand,
And stroll the golden street.

I cased my heart in insulation,
Fenced my will with crosses.
Thus I wait for the Forge of love
And fields where Christ's flock tosses.

My way is just a play on words,
And yet . . . Oh, never mind it—
"Whatever man will lose his life
For Me," God said, "shall find it."